72 Genders

A Comprehensive Guide to Identity

Table of Contents

Disclaimer

The contents of this book on the topic of 72 genders are presented for informational purposes only and do not necessarily reflect the beliefs or views of the author. The author acknowledges that discussions surrounding gender identity and expression are complex and multifaceted, and individuals may hold a wide range of perspectives on these topics.

The author is simply presenting information that is culturally relevant in the USA, with the intention of fostering understanding and dialogue around the diversity of gender identities and experiences. Readers are encouraged to critically engage with the material presented, to seek out diverse perspectives, and to form their own informed opinions based on their own values and beliefs.

In today's rapidly evolving social landscape, the concept of gender has become a focal point of discussion, exploration, and redefinition. Once confined to a binary understanding rooted in biology, gender is now recognized as a multifaceted spectrum encompassing a diverse range of identities, expressions, and experiences. As society grapples with outdated norms and embraces greater inclusivity, the need for comprehensive understanding and appreciation of gender diversity has never been more pressing.

This book serves as a guiding beacon through the complex terrain of gender identity, offering readers a comprehensive toolkit for exploration and understanding. Our journey begins with a foundational overview, where we unpack the very essence of gender and its historical context. From its roots in traditional frameworks to its modern-day complexities, we delve into the myriad factors that shape our understanding of gender and its profound influence on individual lives and societal structures.

At its core, this book is a testament to the power of knowledge and empathy in fostering a more inclusive and equitable world. By providing insights, resources, and real-life narratives, we aim to empower readers to navigate the intricacies of gender with sensitivity and respect. Whether you're a curious newcomer seeking clarity or an ally eager to deepen your understanding, this book offers something for everyone on the journey towards greater gender enlightenment.

As we embark on this exploration together, let us remember the ultimate purpose of our endeavor: to foster understanding and respect for the diverse range of perspectives on gender. While recognizing the complexity of the topic, our goal is to provide insight without necessarily endorsing every perspective. In a world where dialogue and critical thinking are crucial, let us embrace the opportunity to engage with differing viewpoints with open hearts and open minds. With a commitment to empathy and thoughtful inquiry, let us embark on this transformative journey of exploration and understanding, seeking common ground while honoring the complexities of individual experiences.

Acknowledging the diverse nature of gender identities is a fundamental aspect of understanding the complexity of human experience. In today's discourse, there exists a broad spectrum of gender identities beyond the traditional binary framework of male and female. This spectrum encompasses identities such as non-binary, genderqueer, and genderfluid, among others. Each of these identities represents a unique perspective on gender, shaped by individual experiences, cultural influences, and personal understanding.

It's essential to recognize that the existence of diverse gender identities does not inherently imply approval or disapproval. Rather, it reflects the reality of human variation and the fluidity of identity. As we navigate discussions surrounding gender, it's important to approach each perspective with an open mind and a willingness to listen.

By doing so, we can gain a deeper understanding of the complexities of gender and the diverse ways in which it manifests in different individuals' lives.

However, it's equally important to acknowledge that not all perspectives on gender may align with our own beliefs or experiences. While diversity of thought and expression is to be celebrated, it's also essential to engage critically with differing viewpoints. This involves questioning assumptions, examining evidence, and considering the implications of different perspectives on individuals and society as a whole.

Furthermore, the recognition of diverse gender identities does not negate the significance of biological sex or the role it plays in shaping individuals' experiences. Biological sex remains a foundational aspect of human physiology, influencing factors such as reproductive capabilities and hormonal profiles. While gender identity may exist independently of biological sex for some individuals, for others, the two may be closely intertwined.

In exploring the diverse nature of gender identities, it's important to avoid essentializing or oversimplifying complex phenomena. Each individual's experience of gender is unique, shaped by a multitude of factors including but not limited to culture, upbringing, and personal identity. As such, it's crucial to approach discussions of gender with nuance and sensitivity, recognizing the inherent complexity of the topic.

Moreover, while acknowledging the existence of diverse gender identities, it's important to avoid perpetuating harmful stereotypes or assumptions. Conflating gender identity with specific behaviors, interests, or appearances can reinforce rigid gender norms and limit individuals' freedom to express themselves authentically. Instead, we must strive to create spaces that allow for the full expression of gender diversity, free from judgment or prejudice.

Acknowledging the diverse nature of gender identities is essential for fostering understanding and empathy in today's society. However, it's important to approach this recognition with nuance and critical inquiry, avoiding both uncritical acceptance and blanket disapproval. By engaging thoughtfully with differing perspectives and honoring the complexities of individual experiences, we can create a more inclusive and equitable world for all gender identities.

Chapter 1: Understanding Gender

Gender is a multifaceted concept that plays a fundamental role in shaping individuals' identities and experiences within society. At its core, gender refers to the socially constructed roles, behaviors, attributes, and expectations that a particular society considers appropriate for individuals based on their perceived sex. This definition emphasizes the fluid and culturally contingent nature of gender, highlighting that it is not determined solely by biological factors but is also influenced by social, cultural, and historical contexts.

It is crucial to distinguish between sex and gender, as they are often used interchangeably but denote different aspects of identity. Sex typically refers to the biological characteristics that define individuals as male, female, or intersex based on factors such as anatomy, chromosomes, and reproductive organs. In contrast, gender encompasses the societal norms, roles, and expressions associated with masculinity and femininity, which may or may not align with an individual's assigned sex at birth. While sex is typically binary in medical and biological contexts, with individuals categorized as either male or female, gender is more fluid and encompasses a spectrum of identities beyond the traditional male-female binary.

This distinction between sex and gender is essential for understanding the complexities of human identity and the diverse ways in which individuals experience and express their gender.

For example, while an individual may be assigned male at birth based on their biological sex, their gender identity—how they personally identify and experience their gender—may align more closely with femininity, masculinity, or a non-binary identity that transcends traditional gender categories. Similarly, an individual assigned female at birth may identify as a man, a woman, both, neither, or another gender entirely, reflecting the diversity of human experiences and expressions of gender.

Moreover, gender is not only about one's internal sense of self but also about the social and cultural expectations placed upon individuals based on their perceived gender. These expectations can influence various aspects of life, including behavior, appearance, career choices, and social interactions. For example, societal norms may dictate that men should be assertive, competitive, and emotionally stoic, while women should be nurturing, empathetic, and submissive. However, these norms are not universal and may vary significantly across cultures and historical periods, as well as within different social groups.

Additionally, gender intersects with other social categories, such as race, class, sexuality, and disability, shaping individuals' experiences in complex ways. Intersectionality theory highlights how these intersecting identities can create unique systems of privilege and oppression, influencing access to resources, opportunities, and social power.

For example, transgender people of color may face compounded discrimination and marginalization due to their intersecting identities, experiencing higher rates of violence, unemployment, and housing instability compared to their cisgender counterparts.

In recent years, there has been growing recognition of the limitations of traditional binary conceptions of gender and the need for more inclusive frameworks that acknowledge the diversity of human experiences. This recognition has led to discussions about gender diversity and the recognition of non-binary, genderqueer, and gender-nonconforming identities that exist outside the male-female binary. While some cultures have long recognized multiple genders beyond male and female, such as the hijra community in South Asia or the Two-Spirit tradition among some Indigenous peoples in North America, mainstream Western society is only beginning to grapple with these concepts.

It is essential to approach discussions about gender with sensitivity, empathy, and respect for the diverse experiences of individuals across the gender spectrum. While the concept of 72 genders may not align with everyone's understanding or cultural context, acknowledging the complexity and fluidity of gender can foster greater inclusivity, understanding, and acceptance of all individuals, regardless of their gender identity. By challenging rigid gender norms and embracing gender diversity, we can create a more equitable and inclusive society where everyone is free to express their authentic selves without fear of discrimination or marginalization.

Gender identity, gender expression, and biological sex are interconnected yet distinct aspects of human identity that shape individuals' experiences, perceptions, and interactions within society. Understanding these concepts is essential for promoting inclusivity, respect, and recognition of the diversity of human experiences.

Gender identity refers to an individual's deeply held sense of their own gender, which may or may not align with the sex they were assigned at birth. Unlike biological sex, which is typically binary and based on physical characteristics such as anatomy and chromosomes, gender identity is more complex and can encompass a wide range of identities beyond the traditional male-female binary. For many people, their gender identity aligns with the sex they were assigned at birth, and they identify as cisgender. However, for others, their gender identity may differ from their assigned sex, leading them to identify as transgender, non-binary, genderqueer, or another gender identity entirely.

For transgender individuals, their gender identity does not match the sex they were assigned at birth. For example, a person assigned female at birth may identify and live as a man, while someone assigned male at birth may identify and live as a woman. Non-binary individuals, on the other hand, may identify as neither exclusively male nor exclusively female, or they may fluctuate between different gender identities over time. Gender identity is an internal and deeply personal aspect of self, shaped by a combination of biological, psychological, social, and cultural factors.

It is important to respect and affirm individuals' gender identities and use their chosen names and pronouns to support their sense of self and well-being.

Gender expression refers to the outward manifestation of one's gender identity through behavior, appearance, clothing, hairstyle, voice, and other forms of self-presentation. While gender identity is internal and may not always be visible to others, gender expression is often visible and can be influenced by societal norms, cultural expectations, personal preferences, and individual creativity. Gender expression is highly diverse and can vary widely among individuals, regardless of their gender identity or assigned sex.

Society often imposes narrow and rigid expectations about how individuals should express their gender based on their perceived sex. For example, boys are typically encouraged to be assertive, competitive, and emotionally stoic, while girls are expected to be nurturing, empathetic, and passive. However, these norms are socially constructed and can vary significantly across cultures, historical periods, and social contexts. Gender expression is not inherently linked to one's biological sex or gender identity, and individuals should be free to express themselves in ways that feel authentic and comfortable to them, regardless of societal expectations or stereotypes.

Biological sex refers to the anatomical, chromosomal, hormonal, and reproductive characteristics that categorize individuals as male, female, or intersex.

While sex is often thought of as binary, with individuals classified as either male or female based on physical characteristics such as genitalia, chromosomes, and secondary sex characteristics, the reality is more complex. Intersex individuals are born with variations in sex characteristics that do not fit typical definitions of male or female, such as differences in genitalia, chromosomes, or hormone levels. Intersex is a naturally occurring variation of human biology and is estimated to occur in approximately 1.7% of the population.

It is important to recognize that biological sex is not always straightforward or easily categorized, and it does not determine an individual's gender identity or gender expression. While biological sex may influence certain aspects of an individual's experience, such as reproductive health or medical needs, it is not synonymous with gender. Gender is a social and cultural construct that encompasses a broader range of identities, expressions, and experiences beyond the confines of biological sex.

Moreover, the relationship between biological sex, gender identity, and gender expression is complex and multifaceted. While many people's gender identity aligns with their assigned sex at birth and their gender expression conforms to societal expectations based on that assigned sex, others may experience incongruence between these aspects of their identity. For example, a person assigned female at birth may identify as a man and express their gender through masculine clothing, hairstyles, and behaviors.

Conversely, a person assigned male at birth may identify as non-binary and express their gender through a combination of masculine and feminine traits.

In recent years, there has been increasing recognition of the limitations of binary conceptions of sex and gender and the need for more inclusive frameworks that acknowledge the diversity of human experiences. This recognition has led to greater visibility and acceptance of transgender, non-binary, and gender-diverse individuals, as well as efforts to promote equality, respect, and dignity for all people regardless of their gender identity or expression.

By understanding and respecting the complexities of gender identity, gender expression, and biological sex, we can create more inclusive and supportive environments where all individuals are free to express their authentic selves and live with dignity and respect. Education, awareness, and advocacy are essential tools for challenging stereotypes, combating discrimination, and promoting understanding and acceptance of gender diversity in all its forms.

Throughout history and across cultures, understandings of gender have been shaped by a myriad of factors, including social norms, religious beliefs, political ideologies, and economic structures. These perspectives have varied significantly, reflecting the diverse ways in which different societies have conceptualized and organized gender roles, identities, and expressions.

In many ancient civilizations, including those of Mesopotamia, Egypt, Greece, and Rome, gender roles were often hierarchically structured, with men typically occupying positions of power, authority, and privilege, while women were relegated to subordinate roles within the family and society. These patriarchal societies enforced strict gender norms and expectations, prescribing specific behaviors, roles, and responsibilities based on individuals' perceived sex. Women were often confined to domestic duties, such as caregiving, homemaking, and child-rearing, while men were expected to engage in public life, governance, warfare, and commerce. However, there were variations within these societies, with some cultures affording women greater autonomy, status, and rights than others.

In contrast to patriarchal societies, some indigenous cultures and pre-colonial societies recognized multiple genders beyond the traditional male-female binary. For example, among some Indigenous peoples in North America, the Two-Spirit tradition acknowledged individuals who embodied both masculine and feminine qualities, serving unique spiritual, social, and ceremonial roles within their communities. Similarly, the hijra community in South Asia has a long history dating back thousands of years, with individuals who identify as neither exclusively male nor exclusively female occupying distinct social and religious roles. These examples illustrate the diversity of gender identities and expressions that have existed across different cultures and historical periods.

Religion has also played a significant role in shaping perspectives on gender, often reinforcing and perpetuating traditional gender norms and hierarchies. In many religious traditions, including Christianity, Islam, Judaism, Hinduism, and Buddhism, scriptures, teachings, and religious authorities have been used to justify and uphold gender-based inequalities and discrimination. For example, interpretations of religious texts have been used to justify the subordination of women, restrictions on women's autonomy and agency, and the enforcement of gender-specific roles and behaviors. However, religious interpretations and practices regarding gender have evolved over time, with some religious communities advocating for greater gender equality, inclusivity, and social justice.

The advent of colonialism and imperialism further complicated understandings of gender, as European powers imposed their own cultural, social, and gender norms upon colonized peoples, often erasing or suppressing indigenous gender identities and expressions. Colonial authorities sought to impose binary gender categories based on Western understandings of sex and gender, undermining indigenous concepts of gender diversity and fluidity. This colonization had profound and lasting impacts on indigenous cultures, languages, traditions, and identities, contributing to the marginalization and erasure of non-binary and gender-nonconforming individuals.

In the modern era, movements for gender equality, women's rights, and LGBTQ+ rights have challenged traditional gender norms and hierarchies, advocating for greater recognition, acceptance, and affirmation of diverse gender identities and expressions. The feminist movement, which emerged in the late 19th and early 20th centuries, sought to address women's oppression and achieve gender equality by challenging patriarchal structures and advocating for women's rights, autonomy, and agency. Feminist theories and activism have contributed to greater awareness of the social construction of gender, the intersections of gender with other forms of oppression, and the importance of dismantling gender-based discrimination and violence.

Similarly, LGBTQ+ movements have mobilized to challenge heteronormativity and cisnormativity, advocating for the rights, visibility, and dignity of lesbian, gay, bisexual, transgender, and queer individuals. These movements have pushed for legal protections, anti-discrimination policies, healthcare access, and cultural representation for LGBTQ+ people, challenging societal prejudices and promoting acceptance and affirmation of diverse sexual orientations and gender identities. Intersectional approaches to LGBTQ+ activism recognize the overlapping and intersecting systems of oppression that shape individuals' experiences based on factors such as race, class, ethnicity, disability, and immigration status.

Historical and cultural perspectives on gender have been diverse and complex, shaped by a multitude of factors including social, religious, political, and economic influences.

While patriarchal societies have often enforced rigid gender norms and hierarchies, some indigenous cultures have recognized and honored gender diversity beyond the traditional male-female binary. Religion has played a significant role in shaping attitudes towards gender, often reinforcing traditional gender roles and inequalities. Colonialism and imperialism have further complicated understandings of gender by imposing Western gender norms upon colonized peoples, erasing indigenous gender identities and expressions. However, modern movements for gender equality, women's rights, and LGBTQ+ rights have challenged traditional gender norms and advocated for greater recognition, acceptance, and affirmation of diverse gender identities and expressions. Through education, activism, and advocacy, there is potential to create a more inclusive and equitable society where all individuals are free to express their authentic selves without fear of discrimination or marginalization.

Chapter 2: Traditional Gender Categories

Traditional gender categories have long been entrenched in societies worldwide, forming the foundation upon which social norms, cultural expectations, and individual identities are constructed. At the heart of these categories lies the binary distinction between male and female, a dichotomy that has shaped perceptions of gender for centuries. Yet, within this seemingly rigid framework, there exists a rich tapestry of history, culture, and complexity that illuminates the diverse ways in which gender has been understood and expressed across time and geography.

The concept of male and female as distinct genders is deeply rooted in biology, with characteristics such as anatomy, chromosomes, and reproductive functions often serving as the basis for categorization. From a biological standpoint, males typically possess reproductive organs such as testes and external genitalia, while females have ovaries and internal reproductive structures like the uterus. These physiological differences have historically been used to delineate gender roles and expectations within societies, with males often associated with strength, leadership, and aggression, and females with nurturing, caregiving, and domesticity.

Yet, traditional gender categories extend far beyond mere biological distinctions, encompassing a complex web of cultural, social, and psychological factors that shape individuals' experiences and identities. In many cultures, gender roles are deeply ingrained and highly prescriptive, dictating behaviors, appearances, and societal roles based on one's assigned gender at birth.

Boys may be encouraged to be stoic, adventurous, and assertive, while girls are taught to be nurturing, empathetic, and compliant. These gendered expectations permeate every aspect of life, from education and employment to family dynamics and interpersonal relationships.

Throughout history, traditional gender categories have been reinforced and perpetuated through various means, including religion, mythology, folklore, and literature. Myths and legends often feature archetypal characters that embody stereotypical gender traits and behaviors, such as the brave hero or the virtuous maiden. Religious texts and teachings have also played a significant role in shaping gender norms and roles, with many traditions prescribing specific roles and behaviors for men and women based on divine mandates or cultural interpretations of scripture.

Art and media have likewise played a crucial role in perpetuating traditional gender categories, portraying idealized images of masculinity and femininity that reinforce societal norms and expectations. From classical sculptures to modern advertising, depictions of gender have often been idealized and exaggerated, presenting narrow and unrealistic standards of beauty, strength, and desirability. These representations not only reflect societal attitudes towards gender but also influence individuals' perceptions of themselves and others, shaping their self-concept, aspirations, and behaviors.

Despite their pervasive influence, traditional gender categories are not static or universally accepted. Throughout history, there have been countless examples of individuals and communities challenging and subverting traditional gender norms, expressing their gender identities and experiences in ways that defy societal expectations. For example, the phenomenon of cross-dressing has existed in various cultures and historical periods, with individuals donning clothing typically associated with the opposite gender as a form of self-expression, performance, or protest. Similarly, the concept of third genders or gender-nonconforming identities has been recognized in many indigenous cultures, providing space for individuals who do not fit neatly into the binary categories of male and female.

In recent years, there has been growing recognition of the limitations of traditional binary gender categories and the need for more inclusive and expansive understandings of gender. Movements for gender equality, LGBTQ+ rights, and social justice have challenged traditional gender norms and advocated for greater acceptance and affirmation of diverse gender identities and expressions. Non-binary, genderqueer, and gender-fluid identities have gained visibility and recognition, challenging the notion that gender is strictly binary and immutable.

Traditional gender categories have shaped societies and individuals in profound ways, influencing everything from cultural norms and social institutions to personal identities and self-perceptions.

While the binary distinction between male and female has been deeply ingrained in many cultures, it is essential to recognize the complexity and diversity of gender beyond this binary framework. By acknowledging and celebrating the multiplicity of gender identities and expressions, we can create a more inclusive and equitable society where all individuals are free to express their authentic selves without fear of judgment or discrimination.

In examining societal expectations and stereotypes associated with binary genders, it becomes evident how deeply ingrained these norms are within our cultural fabric. From a young age, individuals are socialized into specific roles and behaviors based on their assigned gender, perpetuating a cycle of reinforcement that can be difficult to break free from. For those identified as male, expectations often revolve around notions of strength, stoicism, and assertiveness. Boys are encouraged to be competitive, tough, and unemotional, with vulnerability often seen as a sign of weakness. This pressure to conform to rigid masculine ideals can be stifling, limiting emotional expression and hindering authentic self-expression. Similarly, societal expectations of femininity often emphasize traits such as nurturing, empathy, and compliance. Girls are socialized to prioritize relationships, caretaking, and appearance, with assertiveness and ambition sometimes perceived as undesirable or threatening. These narrow definitions of masculinity and femininity not only constrain individual expression but also perpetuate harmful stereotypes and inequalities.

Moreover, societal expectations of binary genders extend beyond individual behavior to encompass various aspects of life, including education, career choices, and interpersonal relationships. In educational settings, boys may be steered towards STEM fields and competitive sports, while girls are encouraged to pursue humanities, arts, and caregiving professions. These gendered expectations can influence academic and career trajectories, perpetuating disparities in male-dominated and female-dominated fields. In the workplace, gender biases and stereotypes can impact hiring decisions, promotion opportunities, and salary negotiations, with women often facing discrimination and barriers to advancement. Additionally, in personal relationships, traditional gender roles and expectations can shape dynamics around household chores, childcare, and emotional labor, reinforcing unequal power dynamics and limiting individuals' autonomy and fulfillment.

The media plays a significant role in perpetuating and reinforcing societal expectations and stereotypes associated with binary genders. From advertising and entertainment to news media and literature, depictions of masculinity and femininity are often idealized, exaggerated, and stereotypical. Men are portrayed as strong, dominant, and successful, while women are depicted as passive, nurturing, and sexually objectified. These narrow representations not only reinforce gender norms but also contribute to unrealistic standards of beauty, behavior, and achievement. Furthermore, the lack of diverse and authentic representations of gender in media can marginalize and erase the experiences of LGBTQ+ individuals, perpetuating stigma and invisibility.

The intersection of gender with other social categories, such as race, class, sexuality, and disability, further complicates societal expectations and stereotypes associated with binary genders. For example, stereotypes of hypermasculinity and machismo may disproportionately affect men of color, perpetuating harmful narratives of criminality and aggression. Similarly, gendered expectations of caregiving and emotional labor may place additional burdens on women from low-income backgrounds, exacerbating inequalities in access to resources and opportunities. Moreover, individuals who deviate from traditional gender norms, such as transgender and gender-nonconforming people, may face heightened stigma, discrimination, and violence due to their perceived deviation from societal expectations.

In recent years, there has been growing recognition of the limitations and harms of societal expectations and stereotypes associated with binary genders, fueling movements for gender equality, LGBTQ+ rights, and social justice. These movements seek to challenge traditional gender norms and advocate for greater acceptance and affirmation of diverse gender identities and expressions. By raising awareness, promoting education, and advocating for policy change, we can work towards creating a more inclusive and equitable society where all individuals are free to express their authentic selves without fear of judgment or discrimination.

The binary model of gender, which traditionally recognizes only two distinct categories—male and female—has long been the dominant framework through which societies understand and organize gender. However, upon closer examination, it becomes apparent that this binary model is not only restrictive but also fails to fully capture the complexity and diversity of human experiences and identities.

One of the primary limitations of the binary model is its failure to account for the rich diversity of gender identities and expressions that exist beyond the traditional male-female dichotomy. For many individuals, their gender identity does not neatly align with the sex they were assigned at birth, leading them to identify as transgender, non-binary, genderqueer, or another gender identity entirely. These identities challenge the notion that gender is strictly binary and immutable, highlighting the fluidity and complexity of human experiences.

Moreover, the binary model reinforces and perpetuates harmful stereotypes and expectations associated with masculinity and femininity, which can be deeply limiting and restrictive for individuals. For those who identify as male, societal expectations often revolve around notions of strength, dominance, and emotional stoicism, discouraging vulnerability and authentic self-expression. Similarly, for those who identify as female, expectations may center on nurturing, passivity, and physical appearance, placing undue pressure on individuals to conform to narrow and unrealistic standards of femininity.

These rigid gender norms not only constrain individual expression but also contribute to inequality, discrimination, and violence against those who deviate from them.

Furthermore, the binary model fails to account for the intersecting nature of gender with other social categories, such as race, class, sexuality, and disability. Individuals' experiences of gender are shaped by a complex interplay of factors, including their cultural background, socioeconomic status, sexual orientation, and physical ability. For example, stereotypes of hypermasculinity may disproportionately affect men of color, perpetuating harmful narratives of aggression and criminality. Similarly, gendered expectations of caregiving and emotional labor may place additional burdens on women from low-income backgrounds, exacerbating inequalities in access to resources and opportunities. By ignoring these intersections, the binary model overlooks the unique experiences and challenges faced by marginalized and underrepresented communities.

Furthermore, the binary model fails to recognize the existence of non-binary and gender-nonconforming identities that transcend traditional gender categories. Non-binary individuals, for example, may identify as neither exclusively male nor exclusively female, or they may fluctuate between different gender identities over time. Similarly, gender-nonconforming individuals may express their gender in ways that defy societal expectations and stereotypes, challenging the notion that gender is fixed and immutable.

These identities and experiences highlight the limitations of the binary model and underscore the importance of recognizing and affirming the diversity of gender identities and expressions.

There has been growing recognition of the limitations of the binary model and a shift towards more inclusive and expansive understandings of gender. Movements for gender equality, LGBTQ+ rights, and social justice have challenged traditional gender norms and advocated for greater acceptance and affirmation of diverse gender identities and expressions. Non-binary, genderqueer, and gender-fluid identities have gained visibility and recognition, challenging the notion that gender is strictly binary and immutable. By embracing these diverse identities and experiences, we can create a more inclusive and equitable society where all individuals are free to express their authentic selves without fear of judgment or discrimination.

Chapter 3: Beyond the Binary: Non-Binary Identities

Gender is often thought of as a binary concept, with individuals categorized as either male or female. However, this binary understanding fails to encapsulate the diverse range of experiences and identities that exist within the spectrum of gender. Non-binary identities challenge the notion that gender is strictly limited to these two categories, instead recognizing and affirming the existence of identities that fall outside of this binary framework.

At its core, non-binary refers to genders that are not exclusively male or female. People who identify as non-binary may experience their gender as fluid, existing beyond the traditional categories of man or woman. Some may describe their gender as a combination of both, while others may identify with neither. Non-binary identities can encompass a wide array of experiences, feelings, and expressions that do not conform to societal expectations or norms surrounding gender.

One key aspect of non-binary identities is the recognition of gender diversity. Non-binary individuals may use various terms to describe their gender identity, such as genderqueer, agender, bigender, genderfluid, and more. These terms reflect the nuanced ways in which people experience and understand their gender, highlighting the complexity and richness of gender identity beyond the binary.

For many non-binary individuals, their gender identity is deeply personal and may evolve over time. Some may experience a sense of gender dysphoria, discomfort, or distress related to the misalignment between their assigned sex at birth and their true gender identity. Exploring and embracing a non-binary identity can be a journey of self-discovery and self-acceptance, often involving introspection, education, and support from peers and community.

Non-binary identities have existed across cultures and throughout history, challenging the notion that gender is fixed and immutable. Indigenous cultures around the world have long recognized and respected gender diversity, acknowledging the presence of Two-Spirit, hijra, fa'afafine, and other gender identities outside of the Western binary framework. However, non-binary identities have gained increased visibility and recognition in recent years, thanks in part to the efforts of activists, artists, and advocates who are working to amplify non-binary voices and experiences.

In many societies, non-binary individuals face unique challenges and barriers to acceptance. Discrimination, prejudice, and misunderstanding may contribute to feelings of marginalization and exclusion within both LGBTQ+ communities and society at large. Non-binary people may encounter difficulties accessing gender-affirming healthcare, navigating legal documentation, and finding inclusive spaces where their identities are respected and affirmed.

Despite these challenges, non-binary individuals continue to assert their identities and demand recognition, rights, and dignity. Advocacy efforts aimed at challenging gender norms, promoting inclusivity, and centering the voices of non-binary people have contributed to greater awareness and acceptance of non-binary identities. Organizations, institutions, and policymakers are increasingly recognizing the importance of affirming gender diversity and implementing policies and practices that respect and protect the rights of non-binary individuals.

Non-binary identities represent a vital and integral part of the diverse tapestry of human experience. By embracing and affirming non-binary identities, we move closer to creating a world where everyone is free to express their gender authentically and without fear of discrimination or prejudice. As we continue to challenge binary thinking and expand our understanding of gender, we pave the way for a more inclusive and equitable society for all.

Explanation of Non-Binary Terms

Non-binary identities encompass a diverse range of experiences and expressions that fall outside the traditional binary framework of male and female. Understanding the terminology associated with non-binary identities is crucial for fostering inclusivity and affirming the identities of individuals who do not conform to binary gender norms. Here, we explore several key terms used to describe non-binary identities, each reflecting the nuanced ways in which people experience and understand gender.

Genderqueer is a term often used by individuals whose gender identity does not fit within the binary categories of male or female. People who identify as genderqueer may experience their gender as fluid, encompassing elements of both masculinity and femininity, or rejecting these concepts altogether. Genderqueer individuals may express their gender in a variety of ways, challenging societal expectations and norms surrounding gender presentation.

Agender individuals identify as having no gender or experiencing a lack of gender altogether. For agender people, the concept of gender may feel irrelevant or inconsequential to their sense of self. While some agender individuals may experience a sense of neutrality or absence of gender, others may actively reject the notion of gender as a meaningful aspect of identity. Agender people may choose to present themselves in a way that is free from gendered expectations or may explore alternative forms of self-expression.

Bigender individuals experience two distinct gender identities, either simultaneously or at different times. These identities may be binary (male and female), non-binary, or a combination thereof. Bigender people may alternate between presenting as male and female, or they may experience both genders simultaneously, incorporating elements of each into their identity. The experience of being bigender is highly individual and may vary widely among individuals who identify with this term.

Genderfluidity refers to a gender identity that is not fixed or static, but rather changes over time or in different contexts. Genderfluid individuals may experience shifts in their gender identity, expression, or presentation, moving between masculine, feminine, or non-binary genders. These fluctuations may be influenced by factors such as mood, environment, or personal circumstances. Genderfluid people may embrace their fluidity as an integral aspect of their identity, navigating and exploring the diverse facets of gender expression.

Demigender is a term used to describe individuals who partially identify with a particular gender while also identifying with another or with a non-binary identity. Demigender people may experience a strong connection to one gender while feeling only partially aligned with it, or they may identify with a combination of genders. For example, a demigirl may identify partially as female while also feeling a connection to non-binary or other gender identities. Demigender identities highlight the complexity and fluidity of gender experiences beyond the binary.

Neutrois is a term used by individuals who identify as having a neutral or neutral-leaning gender identity. Neutrois people may experience a sense of genderlessness or neutrality, existing outside of the traditional binary categories of male and female. This term emphasizes the rejection of gendered expectations and roles, instead embracing a sense of self that is free from gendered constraints. Neutrois individuals may seek to express themselves in ways that reflect their gender-neutral identity, challenging societal norms and expectations surrounding gender presentation.

Non-binary identities encompass a wide range of experiences and expressions that challenge traditional understandings of gender. By embracing and affirming these identities, we acknowledge the diversity and complexity of human experiences beyond the binary. It is essential to respect and validate the identities of non-binary individuals, creating inclusive spaces where everyone can express their gender authentically and without fear of discrimination or prejudice. As awareness and understanding of non-binary identities continue to grow, we move closer to creating a world where all gender identities are recognized, respected, and celebrated.

Personal Narratives and Experiences of Non-Binary Individuals

The journey to understanding and embracing a non-binary identity is deeply personal and unique to each individual. Through personal narratives and experiences, we gain insight into the diverse ways in which people navigate their gender identity beyond the binary. These stories shed light on the challenges, triumphs, and complexities of living authentically in a world that often seeks to enforce rigid gender norms.

One individual's journey towards identifying as non-binary may involve a process of self-discovery and introspection. For Alex, a non-binary person, their journey began with feelings of discomfort and alienation from traditional gender roles and expectations. "Growing up, I never felt like I fit neatly into the categories of male or female," Alex shares. "I struggled to understand why I didn't feel comfortable in my assigned gender, and it wasn't until later in life that I discovered the term non-binary and realized that it resonated with me."

For others, the journey to understanding their non-binary identity may involve a gradual realization or a sudden epiphany. Sam, a non-binary individual, recalls, "I had always felt a disconnect between my assigned gender and how I saw myself. It wasn't until I stumbled upon stories of other non-binary people online that everything clicked into place for me. Suddenly, I had the language to describe my experiences and the validation to embrace my true identity."

Navigating relationships and social interactions as a non-binary person can present its own set of challenges. Maya, who identifies as non-binary, reflects on their experiences coming out to friends and family. "Coming out as non-binary was both liberating and terrifying," Maya shares. "While I felt relieved to finally be honest about who I am, I also faced skepticism and misunderstanding from some loved ones. It's an ongoing process of education and advocacy, both for myself and for those around me."

Finding acceptance and affirmation within LGBTQ+ communities can also be a significant aspect of the non-binary experience. Kai, a non-binary individual, recounts their journey of finding community and support. "Connecting with other non-binary folks has been incredibly empowering for me," Kai says. "Being able to share experiences, offer support, and celebrate our identities together has been invaluable. It's a reminder that we're not alone in this journey and that our identities are valid and worthy of recognition."

Gender dysphoria, or the distress caused by the misalignment between one's assigned gender and their true gender identity, is a common experience for many non-binary individuals. "For years, I struggled with feelings of dysphoria and discomfort with my body," recalls Taylor, a non-binary person. "It took therapy, self-reflection, and a lot of self-compassion to come to terms with my identity and find ways to alleviate my dysphoria. It's an ongoing process, but embracing my non-binary identity has been transformative for my mental health and well-being."

Non-binary individuals may also face unique challenges when it comes to accessing healthcare and navigating legal documentation. "Finding healthcare providers who understand and respect my identity can be a challenge," says Jordan, a non-binary person. "From finding a therapist who specializes in gender identity to navigating hormone therapy and surgeries, the healthcare system can feel daunting and overwhelming at times. It's crucial for healthcare providers to receive education and training on non-binary identities to ensure that all individuals receive the care and support they need."

Despite the challenges they may face, non-binary individuals continue to assert their identities and advocate for greater visibility and recognition. "I'm proud to be non-binary, and I'm committed to fighting for a world where everyone's gender identity is respected and affirmed," says Avery, a non-binary activist. "Whether it's advocating for inclusive policies, challenging societal norms, or simply living authentically, every act of visibility and resistance helps pave the way for a more equitable and inclusive society."

The personal narratives and experiences of non-binary individuals highlight the richness, diversity, and resilience of gender identity beyond the binary. By sharing their stories, non-binary people challenge stereotypes, break down barriers, and inspire others to embrace their authentic selves. As we continue to listen, learn, and uplift non-binary voices, we move closer to creating a world where everyone can live authentically and without fear of judgment or discrimination based on their gender identity.

Chapter 4: Gender Diversity Across Cultures

Exploring Gender Diversity in Various Cultures and Societies

Gender diversity is a multifaceted concept that is observed across different cultures and civilizations worldwide. Throughout history and in contemporary societies, the understanding and expression of gender have been influenced by a myriad of cultural, social, and historical factors. By examining gender diversity across cultures, we can gain a deeper understanding of the varied ways in which individuals navigate and understand their gender identities, regardless of binary norms.

Indigenous cultures across the globe provide rich examples of gender diversity that challenge Western-centric notions of gender binary. Among Indigenous North American tribes, the concept of Two-Spirit encompasses a spectrum of gender identities beyond traditional male and female roles. Two-Spirit individuals hold unique roles within their communities, often serving as mediators or spiritual leaders. Similarly, in South Asia, the hijra community has a longstanding cultural presence, with members occupying distinct social roles and contributing to various aspects of community life.

In the Pacific Islands, cultures such as Samoa and Tonga recognize gender identities such as fa'afafine and fakaleiti, which defy Western conceptions of gender binary. These individuals, assigned male at birth but embodying feminine roles and expressions, play significant social roles within their communities.

These cultural examples illustrate the diverse ways in which gender is understood and expressed outside of Western norms, challenging mainstream perceptions of gender identity.

Across different cultures, gender diversity is often reflected in language, mythology, and social customs. For example, Hindu mythology includes stories of characters like Shikhandi, who challenges traditional gender roles by living as a different gender than assigned at birth. Similarly, in the Bugis society of Indonesia, the concept of five genders reflects a nuanced understanding of gender diversity beyond the binary. These cultural narratives highlight the fluidity and complexity of gender identity across various societies.

In contemporary Western societies, there is increasing recognition of gender diversity, accompanied by efforts to create more inclusive spaces for individuals of all gender identities. LGBTQ+ movements have played a crucial role in advocating for visibility, acceptance, and rights for non-binary and transgender individuals. Efforts such as the adoption of gender-neutral language and the expansion of gender-affirming healthcare options aim to address the needs of diverse gender identities.

Despite progress, challenges persist for gender-diverse individuals, including stigma, discrimination, and violence. Disparities in healthcare, education, and employment disproportionately affect transgender and non-binary individuals, particularly those from marginalized communities. These challenges underscore the importance of ongoing advocacy and support for gender-diverse individuals.

These cultural examples illustrate the diverse ways in which gender is understood and expressed outside of Western norms, challenging mainstream perceptions of gender identity.

The exploration of gender diversity across cultures highlights the intricate and varied ways in which individuals understand and express their gender identities. By acknowledging and respecting cultural perspectives on gender, we can foster greater understanding and acceptance of gender diversity worldwide. Building inclusive societies requires recognizing the diverse experiences of individuals across cultures and working towards equity and justice for all gender identities.

Examples of Cultures with More Than Two Recognized Genders

Throughout history and across diverse cultures, the concept of gender has been understood in ways that transcend the binary framework of male and female. From ancient civilizations to contemporary societies, numerous cultures have recognized and embraced the existence of more than two genders, reflecting the complexity and diversity of human experiences. Here, we explore fascinating examples of cultures with rich traditions of gender diversity, each offering unique insights into alternative understandings of gender identity.

1. The Bugis Society of Indonesia: The Bugis people, who primarily inhabit the South Sulawesi region of Indonesia, have a cultural tradition that recognizes five distinct genders. Known as "Calabai," "Calalai," "Bissu," "Oroane," and "Makkunrai," these genders encompass a spectrum of identities that defy Western notions of gender binary. The "Bissu," for example, are revered as spiritual leaders who embody both male and female characteristics, serving as intermediaries between the earthly and divine realms. This rich cultural tradition reflects a nuanced understanding of gender diversity that has been celebrated within Bugis society for centuries.

2. The Navajo Nation: Within the Navajo (Diné) culture of the Southwestern United States, the concept of gender extends beyond the binary categories of male and female. The Navajo recognize a third gender known as "Nadleehi," which encompasses individuals who possess both masculine and feminine qualities. Nadleehi individuals play important ceremonial roles within Navajo society, serving as mediators and healers. This cultural acceptance of gender diversity reflects the Navajo's deep connection to their ancestral traditions and spiritual beliefs.

3. The Sworn Virgins of Albania: In the mountainous regions of Albania, there exists a unique cultural phenomenon known as the "Sworn Virgins." Traditionally, if a family lacked a male heir, a designated female would take on the role of a man, assuming male privileges and responsibilities. This decision, known as "becoming a man in the eyes of the law," allowed the sworn virgin to participate in activities typically reserved for men, such as owning property and making decisions for the family.

While the sworn virgin lifestyle is becoming less common due to social and economic changes, it remains a testament to the fluidity of gender roles in Albanian society.

4. The Fa'afafine of Samoa: In Samoan culture, the term "Fa'afafine" refers to individuals who are assigned male at birth but embody both masculine and feminine qualities. Fa'afafine individuals occupy a unique social role within Samoan society, often serving as caregivers, confidants, and community leaders. Unlike Western notions of transgender identity, the Fa'afafine experience is not necessarily tied to gender dysphoria but is rather accepted as a natural expression of gender diversity within Samoan culture. The Fa'afafine exemplify the fluidity and acceptance of gender diversity in Pacific Island cultures.

5. The Guevedoces of the Dominican Republic: In certain regions of the Dominican Republic, there exists a cultural understanding of gender that challenges Western binary norms. Referred to as "Guevedoces," which translates to "penis at 12," individuals born with ambiguous genitalia are initially assigned female at birth. However, during puberty, they undergo a masculinizing transformation due to a deficiency in the enzyme 5-alpha-reductase. As a result, Guevedoces develop male secondary sexual characteristics, including the growth of a penis. This unique cultural phenomenon sheds light on the complexity of gender development and the ways in which cultural beliefs shape understandings of gender identity.

While the sworn virgin lifestyle is becoming less common due to social and economic changes, it remains a testament to the fluidity of gender roles in Albanian society.

These examples represent just a few of the many cultures around the world that recognize and celebrate gender diversity beyond the binary. From the Bugis society of Indonesia to the Navajo Nation of the United States, each culture offers valuable insights into alternative understandings of gender identity and expression. By acknowledging and respecting diverse cultural perspectives on gender, we can foster greater understanding and acceptance of gender diversity worldwide.

Discussion on How Cultural Context Shapes Understandings of Gender

Cultural context plays a profound role in shaping understandings of gender, influencing everything from societal norms and expectations to individual identity and expression. Across different cultures and civilizations, perceptions of gender vary widely, reflecting the unique histories, traditions, and belief systems of each society. By examining the ways in which cultural context shapes understandings of gender, we can gain insight into the complex and dynamic nature of gender identity and expression.

One of the fundamental ways in which cultural context shapes understandings of gender is through the establishment of gender roles and expectations.

From a young age, individuals are socialized into specific roles and behaviors based on their perceived gender, with cultural norms dictating what is considered appropriate or acceptable for males and females. These gender roles can vary significantly from one culture to another, with some societies placing greater emphasis on traditional gender roles, while others may allow for more flexibility and fluidity in gender expression. For example, in some cultures, men may be expected to fulfill roles as providers and protectors, while women are often assigned caregiving and domestic duties. These cultural expectations not only influence individual behavior but also shape broader social structures and institutions.

Religious and spiritual beliefs also play a significant role in shaping cultural understandings of gender. Many cultures draw on religious texts, traditions, and teachings to inform their views on gender identity and expression. In some religious traditions, gender is understood as a binary concept, with strict guidelines for how men and women are expected to behave and interact with one another. However, other religious traditions embrace more nuanced and inclusive understandings of gender, recognizing the existence of diverse gender identities beyond the binary. For example, certain indigenous cultures incorporate gender-diverse deities and spiritual practices into their religious traditions, reflecting a holistic understanding of gender as a multifaceted and sacred aspect of human experience.

Historical and political factors also shape cultural understandings of gender, with colonialism, imperialism, and globalization playing significant roles in shaping contemporary attitudes towards gender identity and expression. The imposition of Western norms and values during periods of colonization has had a profound impact on indigenous cultures and their traditional understandings of gender. Many indigenous societies that once embraced gender diversity were subjected to colonial laws and policies that sought to enforce Western binary gender norms. As a result, some cultural practices and traditions related to gender diversity were suppressed or erased, contributing to the marginalization of gender-diverse individuals within their own communities.

Language and communication also reflect cultural understandings of gender, with different languages encoding gender in various ways. Some languages, such as English, use gendered pronouns and grammatical structures that reinforce binary understandings of gender. In contrast, other languages may have grammatical gender systems that include multiple categories beyond male and female. For example, languages like Spanish and French use gendered nouns and adjectives, with masculine and feminine forms for describing people and objects. However, some languages, such as Swahili and Finnish, do not have grammatical gender distinctions, allowing for greater linguistic flexibility in expressing gender identity.

Art, literature, and media also play a crucial role in shaping cultural understandings of gender, with representations of gender diversity reflecting and perpetuating societal norms and values. Mainstream media often reinforces traditional gender stereotypes and binary norms, perpetuating harmful tropes and erasing the experiences of gender-diverse individuals. However, alternative forms of media, such as independent films, literature, and online communities, offer platforms for marginalized voices to share their stories and challenge dominant narratives surrounding gender identity and expression. By amplifying diverse perspectives and experiences, these forms of media contribute to greater visibility and acceptance of gender diversity within society.

Cultural context profoundly shapes understandings of gender, influencing everything from societal norms and expectations to individual identity and expression. Through the lens of culture, we can better understand the diverse ways in which gender is understood and experienced across different societies and civilizations. By recognizing and respecting cultural perspectives on gender, we can work towards creating more inclusive and equitable societies where everyone's gender identity is affirmed and celebrated.

Chapter 5: Exploring the 72 Genders

Agender: A person who does not identify themselves with or experience any gender. Agender people are also called null-gender, genderless, gendervoid, or neutral gender.

Definition and Characteristics:
Agender individuals, also known as gender-neutral or genderless, do not align themselves with any gender identity. They may feel a sense of detachment from the concept of gender altogether, experiencing themselves as simply human beings without the need for gender labels. This lack of gender identity can be intrinsic to their sense of self, with agender individuals often feeling more comfortable expressing themselves in ways that defy traditional gender norms.

Common Experiences and Challenges:
One of the common experiences of agender individuals is the struggle to navigate a world that often revolves around gender. From filling out forms that require gender identification to facing societal expectations based on gender norms, agender people may find themselves feeling misunderstood or invalidated in their identity. They may also face challenges within interpersonal relationships, as others may struggle to understand or accept their lack of gender identity.

For some agender individuals, coming to terms with their identity can be a liberating experience, allowing them to embrace their authentic selves fully. However, others may struggle with feelings of isolation or alienation, particularly if they feel marginalized within both LGBTQ+ and cisgender communities.

Personal Anecdotes or Testimonials:
"I realized I was agender when I noticed that I never really felt connected to any specific gender identity. Growing up, I always felt like an outsider when it came to gendered expectations and roles. Embracing my agender identity has been a journey of self-discovery and self-acceptance, allowing me to live authentically without the constraints of gender labels."

"I've faced many challenges as an agender individual, from having to explain my identity to skeptical family members to navigating public spaces where gender is constantly reinforced. However, I've also found a sense of freedom in embracing my agender identity. I no longer feel confined by societal expectations or pressured to conform to gender norms that never felt right for me."

Illustrative Examples:
- Sam, an agender individual, prefers to use they/them pronouns and dresses in a way that feels comfortable and authentic to them, regardless of societal expectations based on gender.
- Alex, another agender person, finds joy in expressing themselves through hobbies and interests that have nothing to do with gender, such as painting or playing musical instruments.
- Jamie identifies as agender and has found a supportive community online where they can connect with others who share similar experiences and challenges.

Abimegender: Associated with being profound, deep, and infinite. The term abimegender may be used alone or in combination with other genders.

Definition and Characteristics:
Abimegender is a gender identity characterized by a deep and profound sense of self, often feeling infinite or boundless. Individuals who identify as abimegender may experience their gender as an integral part of their identity, one that transcends traditional binary or even non-binary categories. The term "abime" is derived from the French word "abîme," meaning abyss or chasm, symbolizing the depth and complexity of this gender identity.

Abimegender individuals may feel a deep connection to their gender identity, viewing it as a fundamental aspect of their being that cannot be easily defined or confined by conventional labels. This sense of profundity and infinity can manifest in various ways, from a fluidity in gender expression to a profound introspection about the nature of identity itself.

Common Experiences and Challenges:
One common experience for abimegender individuals is the challenge of articulating and explaining their gender identity to others. Because abimegender is not widely recognized or understood, individuals may face skepticism or disbelief from both within and outside of LGBTQ+ communities. Additionally, navigating societal expectations and norms related to gender can be challenging, as abimegender individuals may feel pressure to conform to binary gender roles or expectations.

Despite these challenges, many abimegender individuals find a sense of empowerment and authenticity in embracing their unique gender identity. For some, the depth and complexity of their gender identity serve as a source of strength and resilience, allowing them to navigate the world with a profound sense of self-awareness and acceptance.

Personal Anecdotes or Testimonials:
"I first discovered the term abimegender while exploring different gender identities online, and it immediately resonated with me. For as long as I can remember, I've felt a deep sense of connection to my gender that goes beyond conventional categories. Embracing my abimegender identity has allowed me to embrace the depth and complexity of who I am without feeling constrained by societal expectations."

"Identifying as abimegender has been both liberating and challenging. While I feel a profound sense of self-awareness and authenticity in embracing my gender identity, I've also faced skepticism and misunderstanding from others who struggle to grasp the concept. Despite these challenges, I wouldn't trade the depth and complexity of my gender identity for anything."

Illustrative Examples:

Riley identifies as abimegender and describes their gender identity as a constantly evolving journey of self-discovery and introspection. They feel a deep sense of connection to their gender that transcends traditional categories.

Maya, another abimegender individual, experiences their gender as a boundless and infinite aspect of their identity. They find solace and empowerment in embracing the depth and complexity of who they are without feeling the need to conform to societal expectations.

Adamas Gender: A gender that is indefinable or indomitable. People identifying with this gender refuse to be categorized in any particular gender identity.

Definition and Characteristics:
Adamas gender is a gender identity characterized by its indefinable and indomitable nature. Individuals who identify with this gender reject the notion of being categorized within any specific gender identity. The term "adamas" is derived from the Greek word meaning "unconquerable" or "invincible," reflecting the resilience and refusal to conform to societal norms or expectations regarding gender.

Adamas gender individuals may experience their gender identity as fluid, multifaceted, and constantly evolving. They may reject the idea of being confined by traditional gender binaries or labels, embracing the complexity and ambiguity of their gender identity instead.

Common Experiences and Challenges:
One common experience for individuals with adamas gender is the challenge of navigating a world that often operates within strict gender categories.

From filling out forms that require gender identification to facing societal expectations based on gender norms, adamas gender individuals may feel misunderstood or invalidated in their identity. They may also face challenges within both LGBTQ+ and cisgender communities, as others may struggle to understand or accept their refusal to conform to traditional gender labels.

Despite these challenges, many adamas gender individuals find empowerment and liberation in embracing their gender identity. They may feel a sense of freedom in rejecting societal expectations and norms, allowing them to live authentically and true to themselves.

Personal Anecdotes or Testimonials:
"I've never felt comfortable identifying within any specific gender category. For as long as I can remember, I've always felt a sense of ambiguity and fluidity when it comes to my gender identity. Embracing my adamas gender has been a journey of self-discovery and self-acceptance, allowing me to reject societal expectations and live authentically."

"Identifying as adamas gender has its challenges, particularly when others struggle to understand or accept my refusal to conform to traditional gender labels. However, I've also found a sense of empowerment in embracing the complexity and ambiguity of my gender identity. I refuse to be categorized or confined by societal norms, and that refusal is what makes me feel truly invincible."

Illustrative Examples:

Jordan identifies as adamas gender and describes their gender identity as fluid and undefinable. They reject the idea of being categorized within any specific gender label and instead embrace the ambiguity and complexity of their identity.
Taylor, another adamas gender individual, refuses to conform to societal expectations regarding gender. They reject the notion of being confined by traditional gender binaries and find empowerment in embracing the indomitable nature of their gender identity.

Aerogender: Also called evaisgender, this gender identity changes according to one's surroundings.

Definition and Characteristics:
Aerogender, also known as evaisgender, is a gender identity characterized by its fluidity and responsiveness to one's surroundings. Individuals who identify as aerogender may experience shifts or changes in their gender identity based on factors such as their environment, social context, or emotional state. The term "aero" is derived from the Greek word for air, emphasizing the ethereal and ever-changing nature of this gender identity.

Aerogender individuals may feel a sense of connection to the elements or the natural world, with their gender identity shifting in response to changes in their surroundings. This fluidity can manifest in various ways, from feeling more masculine, feminine, or non-binary depending on the people they are with or the spaces they inhabit.

Common Experiences and Challenges:
One common experience for individuals with aerogender is the challenge of navigating a world that often expects consistency and stability in gender identity. Aerogender individuals may struggle with feelings of uncertainty or confusion about their gender identity, particularly if they experience frequent shifts or changes. They may also face challenges in interpersonal relationships, as others may struggle to understand or accept the fluid nature of their gender identity.

Despite these challenges, many aerogender individuals find a sense of freedom and empowerment in embracing the fluidity of their gender identity. They may feel liberated from the constraints of traditional gender categories, allowing them to express themselves authentically and adaptively in different contexts.

Personal Anecdotes or Testimonials:
"I first discovered the term aerogender when I realized that my gender identity seemed to change depending on who I was with and where I was. Sometimes I feel more masculine, other times more feminine, and sometimes neither at all. Embracing my aerogender identity has been a journey of self-discovery and self-acceptance, allowing me to embrace the fluidity of who I am."

"Identifying as aerogender has its challenges, particularly when others struggle to understand or accept the ever-changing nature of my gender identity. However, I've also found a sense of liberation in embracing the fluidity of who I am. I no longer feel confined by rigid gender categories, and that freedom is what allows me to truly be myself."

Illustrative Examples:

Jamie identifies as aerogender and describes their gender identity as shifting like the wind, adapting to different social contexts and environments. They may feel more masculine when surrounded by certain people or more feminine in certain spaces.
Alex, another aerogender individual, experiences their gender identity as fluid and adaptive, changing in response to changes in their surroundings or emotional state. They find empowerment in embracing the ever-changing nature of who they are.

Aesthetigender: Also called aesthetgender, it is a type of gender identity derived from aesthetics.

Definition and Characteristics:
Aesthetigender, or aesthetgender, is a gender identity that is closely tied to aesthetics, beauty, or visual elements. Individuals who identify as aesthetigender may experience their gender as being influenced by or aligned with certain aesthetic qualities, styles, or expressions. This gender identity is often deeply personal and subjective, with individuals deriving a sense of identity and belonging from their aesthetic preferences.

Aesthetigender individuals may feel a strong connection to specific aesthetic concepts, such as minimalism, vintage, or futuristic styles, which may influence their gender expression and identity. The term "aesthetigender" emphasizes the importance of aesthetics in shaping one's sense of self and gender identity.

Common Experiences and Challenges:
One common experience for individuals with aesthetigender is the challenge of navigating a world that often prioritizes binary or rigid gender norms. Aesthetigender individuals may face skepticism or disbelief from both within and outside of LGBTQ+ communities, as others may struggle to understand or accept the connection between aesthetics and gender identity. They may also experience challenges in finding spaces or communities where they feel understood and validated in their identity.

Despite these challenges, many aesthetigender individuals find a sense of empowerment and self-expression in embracing their unique gender identity. They may feel liberated from the constraints of traditional gender categories, allowing them to explore and celebrate their aesthetic preferences freely.

Personal Anecdotes or Testimonials:
"I've always been drawn to certain aesthetic styles and concepts, and I never realized until later in life that these preferences were deeply tied to my gender identity. Embracing my aesthetigender identity has allowed me to fully embrace and express myself in ways that feel authentic and true to who I am."

"Identifying as aesthetigender has its challenges, particularly when others struggle to understand or accept the connection between aesthetics and gender identity. However, I've also found a sense of empowerment and belonging in embracing my unique identity. I no longer feel confined by traditional gender norms, and that freedom is what allows me to fully express myself."

Illustrative Examples:

Riley identifies as aesthetigender and finds a deep sense of connection to vintage aesthetics. They express their gender identity through fashion, decor, and art that reflects their love for all things vintage.
Jordan, another aesthetigender individual, feels most aligned with minimalist aesthetics. They prefer clean lines, simple designs, and neutral colors in their gender expression, finding beauty and comfort in simplicity.

Affectugender: This is based on the person's mood swings or fluctuations.

Definition and Characteristics:
Affectugender is a gender identity that is influenced by a person's mood swings or fluctuations. Individuals who identify as affectugender may experience changes in their gender identity in response to shifts in their emotional state or mood. This gender identity is characterized by its fluidity and responsiveness to internal emotional experiences, with one's gender identity fluctuating along with their mood.

Affectugender individuals may find that their gender identity varies from day to day or even throughout the day, depending on their emotional state. This fluidity can be intrinsic to their sense of self, with their gender identity shifting in response to changes in their mental and emotional well-being.

Common Experiences and Challenges:
One common experience for individuals with affectugender is the challenge of navigating a world that often expects consistency and stability in gender identity. Affectugender individuals may struggle with feelings of uncertainty or confusion about their gender identity, particularly if they experience frequent mood swings or fluctuations. They may also face challenges in interpersonal relationships, as others may struggle to understand or accept the fluid nature of their gender identity.

Despite these challenges, many affectugender individuals find empowerment and liberation in embracing the fluidity of their gender identity. They may feel a sense of freedom in rejecting societal expectations and norms, allowing them to express themselves authentically and adaptively in different emotional states.

Personal Anecdotes or Testimonials:
"I first realized I was affectugender when I noticed that my gender identity seemed to change along with my mood swings. Some days, I feel more masculine, while other days, I feel more feminine or non-binary. Embracing my affectugender identity has been a journey of self-acceptance and self-compassion, allowing me to embrace the fluidity of who I am."

"Identifying as affectugender has its challenges, particularly when others struggle to understand or accept the ever-changing nature of my gender identity.

However, I've also found a sense of liberation in embracing the fluidity of who I am. I no longer feel confined by rigid gender categories, and that freedom is what allows me to truly be myself."

Illustrative Examples:

Jamie identifies as affectugender and describes their gender identity as fluctuating along with their mood swings. They may feel more aligned with certain gender expressions depending on their emotional state at any given time.
Alex, another affectugender individual, experiences their gender identity as fluid and adaptive, changing in response to changes in their mood or emotional well-being. They find empowerment in embracing the ever-changing nature of who they are.

Agenderflux: A person with this gender identity is mostly agender with brief shifts of belonging to other gender types.

Definition and Characteristics:
Agenderflux is a gender identity characterized by being mostly agender, with brief shifts or fluctuations of belonging to other gender types. Individuals who identify as agenderflux may primarily experience themselves as lacking a gender identity (agender), but occasionally experience temporary or fleeting connections to other gender identities. These shifts can vary in intensity and frequency, with some individuals experiencing them more frequently than others.

Agenderflux individuals may find that their gender identity fluctuates over time, with periods of feeling completely agender followed by brief moments of alignment with other gender identities. This fluidity can be intrinsic to their sense of self, with their gender identity shifting along a spectrum of gender experiences.

Common Experiences and Challenges:
One common experience for individuals with agenderflux is the challenge of navigating a world that often expects consistency and stability in gender identity. Agenderflux individuals may struggle with feelings of confusion or uncertainty about their gender identity, particularly during periods of shifting or fluctuation. They may also face challenges in finding language to describe their experiences, as agenderflux is a less widely recognized or understood gender identity.

Despite these challenges, many agenderflux individuals find empowerment and validation in embracing the fluidity of their gender identity. They may feel a sense of freedom in rejecting societal expectations and norms, allowing them to express themselves authentically and adaptively in different gender experiences.

Personal Anecdotes or Testimonials:
"I first realized I was agenderflux when I noticed that my gender identity seemed to fluctuate over time. Most of the time, I feel completely agender, but occasionally I'll experience brief moments of alignment with other gender identities. Embracing my agenderflux identity has been a journey of self-discovery and self-acceptance, allowing me to embrace the fluidity of who I am."

"Identifying as agenderflux has its challenges, particularly when others struggle to understand or accept the fluctuating nature of my gender identity. However, I've also found a sense of liberation in embracing the fluidity of who I am. I no longer feel confined by rigid gender categories, and that freedom is what allows me to truly be myself."

Illustrative Examples:

Riley identifies as agenderflux and describes their gender identity as mostly agender, with occasional shifts of alignment with other gender types. They may experience periods of feeling completely agender followed by brief moments of connection to other gender identities.
Jordan, another agenderflux individual, experiences their gender identity as fluid and adaptive, with their sense of self shifting along a spectrum of gender experiences. They find empowerment in embracing the ever-changing nature of who they are.

Alexigender: The person has a fluid gender identity between more than one type of gender although they cannot name the genders they feel fluid in.

Definition and Characteristics:
Alexigender is a gender identity characterized by fluidity between multiple gender identities, without being able to specifically name or label those genders. Individuals who identify as alexigender may experience shifts or fluctuations in their gender identity, feeling a sense of fluidity between more than one gender identity. However, they may find it difficult or impossible to articulate or define the specific genders they feel fluid in.

Alexigender individuals may experience their gender identity as dynamic and ever-changing, with their sense of self shifting along a spectrum of gender experiences. This fluidity can be intrinsic to their sense of self, with their gender identity evolving over time and in different contexts.

Common Experiences and Challenges:
One common experience for individuals with alexigender is the challenge of navigating a world that often expects clarity and certainty in gender identity. Alexigender individuals may struggle with feelings of ambiguity or uncertainty about their gender identity, particularly if they cannot name or label the genders they feel fluid in. They may also face challenges in finding language to describe their experiences, as alexigender is a less widely recognized or understood gender identity.

Despite these challenges, many alexigender individuals find empowerment and validation in embracing the fluidity of their gender identity. They may feel a sense of freedom in rejecting societal expectations and norms, allowing them to express themselves authentically and adaptively in different gender experiences.

Personal Anecdotes or Testimonials:
"I've always felt a sense of fluidity in my gender identity, shifting between more than one gender without being able to name or label them. Some days, I feel more aligned with certain aspects of masculinity, while other days, I may feel more connected to femininity or non-binary identities.

Embracing my alexigender identity has been a journey of self-discovery and self-acceptance, allowing me to embrace the complexity and fluidity of who I am."

"Identifying as alexigender has its challenges, particularly when others struggle to understand or accept the fluid nature of my gender identity. However, I've also found a sense of liberation in embracing the ever-changing nature of who I am. I no longer feel confined by rigid gender categories, and that freedom is what allows me to truly be myself."

Illustrative Examples:

Riley identifies as alexigender and describes their gender identity as fluid between multiple gender experiences, without being able to specifically name or label those genders. They may feel a sense of liberation in embracing the complexity and fluidity of their identity.
Jordan, another alexigender individual, experiences their gender identity as dynamic and ever-changing, with their sense of self shifting between more than one gender without clear definitions. They find empowerment in embracing the fluidity of who they are.

Aliusgender: Standing Apart from Existing Social Gender Constructs

Definition and Characteristics:
Aliusgender is a gender identity that stands apart from existing social gender constructs. It involves having a strong and specific gender identity that is distinct from both male and female genders.

Individuals who identify as aliusgender may feel a deep sense of connection to their unique gender identity, one that does not fit within the traditional binary framework of male and female.

Characteristics of aliusgender may include a strong internal sense of self that transcends societal gender norms, as well as a feeling of being fundamentally different from conventional gender categories. Aliusgender individuals may experience their gender identity as deeply personal and intrinsic to their sense of self, even if it does not align with societal expectations or norms.

Common Experiences and Challenges:
One common experience for individuals with aliusgender is the challenge of navigating a world that often operates within rigid binary gender constructs. Aliusgender individuals may face invalidation or disbelief from both within and outside of LGBTQ+ communities, as others may struggle to understand or accept a gender identity that falls outside of the traditional male/female binary.

Aliusgender individuals may also experience challenges in finding language to describe their experiences, as aliusgender is a less widely recognized or understood gender identity. They may feel isolated or marginalized within both LGBTQ+ and cisgender communities, as their gender identity may not fit neatly into existing social frameworks.

Despite these challenges, many aliusgender individuals find empowerment and validation in embracing their unique gender identity. They may feel a sense of liberation in rejecting societal expectations and norms, allowing them to express themselves authentically and assert their identity on their own terms.

Illustrative Examples:

Evan: Evan identifies as aliusgender and describes their gender identity as a deeply personal and unique aspect of who they are. They feel a strong sense of connection to their gender identity, even though it does not fit within traditional male or female categories. Evan finds empowerment in embracing their identity and standing apart from existing social gender constructs.
Sam: Sam is another aliusgender individual who experiences their gender identity as distinct from conventional gender categories. Sam feels a sense of liberation in embracing their unique gender identity and rejecting societal expectations. Despite facing challenges and misconceptions from others, Sam finds strength in asserting their identity and standing apart from existing gender norms.

Amaregender: Gender Identity Attached to Emotional Bonds

Definition and Characteristics:
Amaregender is a gender identity that changes depending on the person one is emotionally attached to. Individuals who identify as amaregender may experience shifts or fluctuations in their gender identity based on their emotional connections with others. The term "amare" is derived from the Latin word for love, emphasizing the close relationship between emotional attachment and gender identity.

Characteristics of amaregender may include a sense of fluidity or adaptability in one's gender identity, with one's sense of self shifting in response to changes in emotional bonds. Amaregender individuals may feel a deep sense of connection to their gender identity when in the presence of certain individuals, while experiencing changes or fluctuations when those emotional bonds change or evolve.

Common Experiences and Challenges:
One common experience for individuals with amaregender is the challenge of navigating a world that often expects consistency and stability in gender identity. Amaregender individuals may struggle with feelings of uncertainty or confusion about their gender identity, particularly if they experience frequent shifts or fluctuations based on their emotional connections.

Amaregender individuals may also face challenges in interpersonal relationships, as others may struggle to understand or accept the connection between emotional attachment and gender identity. They may feel pressure to explain or justify their shifting gender identity to others, leading to feelings of invalidation or misunderstanding.

Illustrative Examples:

Chris: Chris identifies as amaregender and experiences their gender identity as closely tied to their emotional bonds with others. When in the presence of their partner, Chris feels a strong sense of alignment with a particular gender identity. However, when apart from their partner or in the presence of others, Chris's gender identity may shift or fluctuate. Despite these challenges, Chris finds validation and affirmation in embracing their unique identity and the close connection between love and gender.

Alex: Another individual, Alex, also identifies as amaregender. Alex experiences their gender identity as fluid and adaptive, changing in response to changes in their emotional attachments with others. Despite facing challenges in explaining their shifting gender identity to others, Alex finds empowerment in embracing the close relationship between emotional bonds and gender identity.

Ambigender: Simultaneous Presence of Two Specific Gender Identities

Definition and Characteristics:
Ambigender is a gender identity characterized by the simultaneous presence of two specific gender identities without any fluidity or fluctuations between them. Individuals who identify as ambigender experience a fixed and stable sense of self with regards to their gender, feeling a strong and consistent connection to two distinct gender identities at the same time. These gender identities may coexist harmoniously within the individual's sense of self, without one identity overpowering or dominating the other.

Characteristics of ambigender may include a deep sense of understanding and acceptance of both gender identities, as well as a feeling of completeness or wholeness in embracing both aspects of their gender identity simultaneously. Ambigender individuals may find empowerment and validation in their unique identity, despite societal expectations for binary or singular gender identities.

Common Experiences and Challenges:
One common experience for individuals with ambigender is the challenge of navigating a world that often expects individuals to fit neatly into binary gender categories. Ambigender individuals may face skepticism or disbelief from both within and outside of LGBTQ+ communities, as others may struggle to understand or accept a gender identity that exists outside of the traditional binary framework.

Ambigender individuals may also experience challenges in finding language to describe their experiences, as ambigender is a less widely recognized or understood gender identity. They may feel pressure to conform to societal expectations or norms, leading to feelings of invisibility or marginalization within both LGBTQ+ and cisgender communities.

Illustrative Examples:

Jordan: Jordan identifies as ambigender and experiences a strong and unwavering connection to both masculinity and femininity simultaneously. They feel a sense of completeness and wholeness in embracing both aspects of their gender identity, despite societal pressures to conform to binary gender norms. Jordan finds empowerment and validation in their unique identity and the harmonious coexistence of two specific gender identities within themselves.

Sam: Another individual, Sam, also identifies as ambigender. Sam experiences a fixed and stable sense of self with regards to their gender, feeling a deep and enduring connection to both masculinity and femininity without any fluidity or fluctuations between them. Despite facing challenges in navigating a world that often expects binary gender identities, Sam finds strength and resilience in embracing their authentic self and the simultaneous presence of two distinct gender identities.

Ambonec: Identifying as Both Man and Woman Yet Belonging to Neither

Definition and Characteristics: Ambonec is a gender identity where an individual identifies themselves as both man and woman, yet they do not feel like they belong to either gender category. This identity is characterized by a sense of being simultaneously connected to aspects of masculinity and femininity, but not fully aligning with either traditional gender role or label. The term "ambonec" reflects the ambiguity and complexity of this gender identity.

Characteristics of ambonec may include a fluid and non-binary sense of self, where the individual feels comfortable expressing both masculine and feminine traits, behaviors, and characteristics. However, despite this duality, they may not feel wholly represented by either the concept of manhood or womanhood.

Common Experiences and Challenges: One common experience for individuals with ambonec identity is the challenge of navigating a world that often operates within rigid binary gender constructs. Ambonec individuals may face invalidation or misunderstanding from both within and outside of LGBTQ+ communities, as others may struggle to comprehend or accept a gender identity that falls outside of the traditional binary.

Ambonec individuals may also experience challenges in finding acceptance and validation for their identity, as it can be less recognized or understood compared to more mainstream gender identities. They may face pressure to conform to societal expectations or norms regarding gender, leading to feelings of isolation or invisibility.

Illustrative Examples:
- Alex: Alex identifies as ambonec and experiences a deep sense of connection to both masculinity and femininity. However, they do not feel wholly represented by either traditional gender category. Despite facing challenges in navigating societal expectations and norms, Alex finds empowerment and validation in embracing their unique gender identity and the fluidity of their sense of self.
- Jordan: Another individual, Jordan, also identifies as ambonec. Jordan feels comfortable expressing both masculine and feminine traits and behaviors but does not feel fully aligned with either traditional gender role. Despite facing challenges in finding acceptance and understanding from others, Jordan finds strength and resilience in embracing their authentic self and the complexity of their gender identity.

Amicagender: Gender Fluidity Based on Social Circles

Definition and Characteristics:
Amicagender is a gender-fluid identity where a person changes their gender depending on the friends they have. Individuals who identify as amicagender may experience shifts or fluctuations in their gender identity based on the social context or the people they are with. The term "amicagender" combines "amica," Latin for friend, with gender, emphasizing the connection between one's gender identity and their social relationships.

Characteristics of amicagender may include a fluid and adaptive sense of self, where the individual feels comfortable expressing different gender identities depending on the social circle or context. This fluidity can manifest in various ways, from changes in gender expression to shifts in how one internally experiences their gender.

Common Experiences and Challenges:
One common experience for individuals with amicagender is the challenge of navigating a world that often expects consistency and stability in gender identity. Amicagender individuals may struggle with feelings of uncertainty or confusion about their gender identity, particularly if they experience frequent shifts or fluctuations based on their social interactions.

Amicagender individuals may also face challenges in finding acceptance and validation for their identity, as it can be less recognized or understood compared to more mainstream gender identities. They may feel pressure to conform to societal expectations or norms regarding gender, leading to feelings of anxiety or insecurity.

Illustrative Examples:

Chris: Chris identifies as amicagender and experiences their gender identity as fluid and adaptive depending on the friends they are with. When spending time with certain friends, Chris may feel more comfortable expressing a certain gender identity, while with others, they may experience a different gender identity. Despite facing challenges in finding acceptance and understanding from others, Chris finds empowerment in embracing their fluid sense of self and the connection between their gender identity and social relationships.
Sam: Another individual, Sam, also identifies as amicagender. Sam experiences shifts in their gender identity based on the social context or the people they are interacting with. Despite facing challenges in navigating societal expectations and norms, Sam finds strength and resilience in embracing their authentic self and the fluidity of their gender identity.

Androgyne: Embracing a Blend of Feminine and Masculine Genders

Definition and Characteristics:
Androgyne is a gender identity where a person feels a combination of both feminine and masculine genders. Individuals who identify as androgyne may experience a sense of balance or harmony between traditionally feminine and masculine qualities within their sense of self. The term "androgyne" is derived from the Greek words for "man" and "woman," reflecting the blending of gender characteristics.

Characteristics of androgyne may include an internal sense of androgyny, where the individual feels comfortable expressing both feminine and masculine traits, behaviors, and characteristics. This can manifest in various ways, including in one's appearance, mannerisms, and self-expression.

Common Experiences and Challenges:
One common experience for individuals with androgyne identity is the challenge of navigating a world that often operates within rigid binary gender constructs. Androgyne individuals may face pressure to conform to traditional gender norms or expectations, leading to feelings of invalidation or misunderstanding. They may also experience discrimination or prejudice from both within and outside of LGBTQ+ communities, as others may struggle to understand or accept a gender identity that exists outside of the binary.

Androgyne individuals may also face challenges in finding acceptance and validation for their identity, as it can be less recognized or understood compared to more mainstream gender identities. They may feel pressure to choose between presenting as either traditionally feminine or masculine, leading to feelings of frustration or confusion.

Illustrative Examples:

Alex: Alex identifies as androgyne and feels a deep sense of connection to both feminine and masculine genders. They express their gender identity through a blend of traditionally feminine and masculine traits, finding empowerment in embracing their androgyny. Despite facing challenges in navigating societal expectations and norms, Alex finds strength in asserting their authentic self and the balance between their feminine and masculine qualities.

Jordan: Another individual, Jordan, also identifies as androgyne. Jordan experiences a sense of harmony between feminine and masculine genders within themselves, feeling comfortable expressing both aspects of their identity. Despite facing challenges in finding acceptance and understanding from others, Jordan finds empowerment in embracing their unique gender identity and the androgynous qualities that define it.

Anesigender: Bridging Comfort and Affinity with Gender Identities

Definition and Characteristics:
Anesigender describes a gender identity where an individual feels close to a specific type of gender while being more comfortable closely identifying with another gender. In essence, the person experiences a sense of affinity or connection to a particular gender identity yet finds greater comfort in aligning themselves with a different gender. This identity emphasizes the complexity and nuanced relationship an individual may have with their gender identity.

Characteristics of anesigender may include a deep internal awareness of the specific gender type they feel close to, alongside a sense of ease and comfort in identifying more closely with another gender identity. This can lead to a dynamic and multifaceted understanding of oneself in relation to gender.

Common Experiences and Challenges:
One common experience for individuals with anesigender identity is the internal conflict or tension that can arise from feeling close to one gender while aligning more closely with another. This internal discord can lead to feelings of confusion, frustration, or a sense of being misunderstood by oneself and others.

Anesigender individuals may also face challenges in navigating social interactions and relationships, particularly when others expect them to align strictly with the gender they feel close to rather than the one they are more comfortable identifying with. This can lead to feelings of pressure to conform to societal expectations or norms, leading to feelings of discomfort or anxiety.

Illustrative Examples:

Chris: Chris identifies as anesigender and feels a strong affinity towards femininity yet finds greater comfort in identifying as non-binary. Despite feeling a connection to femininity, Chris finds that their true sense of self aligns more closely with non-binary identity, leading to a nuanced understanding of themselves in relation to gender.
Sam: Another individual, Sam, also identifies as anesigender. Sam feels drawn to masculinity but feels more comfortable identifying as a woman. Despite feeling close to masculinity, Sam finds that their authentic sense of self is better expressed through a woman's identity, leading to a complex and nuanced relationship with gender.

Angenital: Embracing a Desire for Absence of Primary Sexual Characteristics

Definition and Characteristics:
Angenital describes a unique identity where an individual desires to be without any primary sexual characteristics, such as genitalia, while still maintaining a gender identity. Unlike agender individuals who may not identify with any gender, angenital individuals maintain a sense of gender identity despite their desire for a lack of specific physical attributes. The term "angenital" emphasizes the focus on absence or lack of primary sexual characteristics rather than an absence of gender identity.

Characteristics of angenital may include a deep-seated longing for a body without primary sexual characteristics, alongside a strong and distinct gender identity. Individuals who identify as angenital may experience a sense of disconnect between their gender identity and their physical body, leading to complex feelings and experiences.

Unique Common Experiences and Challenges:
One unique experience for individuals with angenital identity is navigating the intersection of desire for a specific body configuration and maintaining a sense of gender identity. This can lead to internal conflict or tension as they reconcile their desire for physical alteration with their understanding of their own gender identity.

Angenital individuals may also face challenges in accessing medical or surgical interventions to alter their physical characteristics to align with their desired state. This can lead to feelings of frustration or dysphoria as they navigate healthcare systems that may not fully understand or accommodate their unique needs.

Furthermore, angenital individuals may encounter societal misconceptions or stigma surrounding their desire for a body without primary sexual characteristics. They may face invalidation or disbelief from both within and outside of LGBTQ+ communities, as others may struggle to understand or accept their identity and desires.

Despite these challenges, many angenital individuals find strength and resilience in embracing their unique identity and advocating for greater visibility and understanding within broader society.

Illustrative Example:

Jordan: Jordan identifies as angenital and experiences a deep longing to be without any primary sexual characteristics, while still maintaining a strong sense of gender identity as a woman. Despite facing challenges in navigating societal expectations and norms, Jordan finds empowerment in embracing their unique identity and advocating for greater acceptance and understanding of diverse gender experiences.

Anogender: Fluxing Intensity of Gender Identity

Definition and Characteristics:
Anogender describes a gender identity characterized by fluctuations in intensity, where the gender identity fades in and out in strength but consistently returns to the same gendered feeling. Unlike genderfluidity, where individuals experience shifts between different gender identities, those who identify as anogender maintain a consistent gender identity despite variations in its intensity over time. The term "anogender" underscores the cyclical nature of the intensity of the gendered feeling.

Characteristics of anogender may include periods of strong identification with a particular gender, followed by periods of reduced intensity or ambiguity in the strength of that gender identity. Despite these fluctuations, individuals who identify as anogender maintain a consistent core gender identity that remains unchanged throughout these variations.

Common Experiences and Challenges:
One common experience for individuals with anogender identity is the challenge of navigating the fluctuations in the intensity of their gender identity. These fluctuations can lead to feelings of confusion, uncertainty, or instability as individuals grapple with changes in the strength of their gendered feelings over time.

Anogender individuals may also face challenges in maintaining a sense of self and identity amidst these fluctuations. The ebb and flow of the intensity of their gender identity can lead to feelings of disconnection or dysphoria as they navigate periods of reduced identification with their gender.

Additionally, anogender individuals may encounter difficulties in finding language to describe their experiences, as anogender is a less widely recognized or understood gender identity. They may struggle to articulate their feelings and experiences to others, leading to feelings of isolation or invalidation.

Despite these challenges, many anogender individuals find strength and resilience in embracing the complexity of their gender identity and advocating for greater visibility and understanding within broader society.

Illustrative Example:

Jordan: Jordan identifies as anogender and experiences fluctuations in the intensity of their gender identity. There are times when Jordan feels a strong connection to their gender, while at other times, the intensity fades, leading to feelings of uncertainty or ambiguity. Despite these fluctuations, Jordan maintains a consistent core gender identity that remains unchanged throughout these variations. Jordan navigates these challenges with resilience and self-awareness, finding empowerment in embracing the complexity of their gender identity.

Antegender: Embracing a Protean and Formless Gender Identity

Definition and Characteristics:
Antegender describes a gender identity that is protean and formless, capable of being anything yet devoid of specific form or motion. Individuals who identify as antegender may experience their gender identity as fluid and amorphous, lacking distinct attributes or characteristics associated with traditional gender categories. The term "antegender" emphasizes the ever-changing and boundless nature of this gender identity.

Characteristics of antegender may include a sense of liberation and freedom in embracing the fluidity and formlessness of one's gender identity. Antegender individuals may experience a profound sense of self-awareness and acceptance of the limitless possibilities inherent in their gender expression, transcending the confines of societal expectations or norms regarding gender.

Common Experiences and Challenges:
One common experience for individuals with antegender identity is the challenge of navigating a world that often expects individuals to neatly fit into predefined gender categories. Antegender individuals may face pressure to conform to traditional binary notions of gender, leading to feelings of invisibility or invalidation of their unique identity.

Antegender individuals may also encounter difficulties in finding acceptance and validation for their identity, as it can be less recognized or understood compared to more mainstream gender identities. They may struggle to find language to describe their experiences, leading to feelings of isolation or marginalization within both LGBTQ+ and cisgender communities.

Furthermore, antegender individuals may experience challenges in accessing supportive resources or communities that fully embrace and understand the complexity of their gender identity. They may feel disconnected or misunderstood by others who struggle to comprehend the concept of a gender identity that transcends traditional boundaries or categories.

Despite these challenges, many antegender individuals find empowerment and validation in embracing the boundless and formless nature of their gender identity. They may advocate for greater acceptance and understanding of diverse gender experiences within broader society, challenging societal norms and expectations regarding gender in the process.

Illustrative Example:

Jordan: Jordan identifies as antegender and experiences their gender identity as protean and formless, capable of being anything yet devoid of specific attributes or characteristics. They find liberation and freedom in embracing the limitless possibilities inherent in their gender expression, transcending the confines of societal expectations or norms regarding gender.

Despite facing challenges in navigating societal expectations and norms, Jordan finds strength and resilience in asserting their authentic self and advocating for greater acceptance and understanding of diverse gender experiences.

Anxiegender: Gender Identity Defined by Anxiety

Definition and Characteristics:
Anxiegender is a gender identity characterized by anxiety as its prominent characteristic. Individuals who identify as anxiegender experience their gender identity in relation to their anxiety, with feelings of anxiety playing a significant role in shaping their understanding of their gender. The term "anxiegender" underscores the close connection between anxiety and gender identity.

Characteristics of anxiegender may include a profound sense of anxiety surrounding one's gender identity, with feelings of uncertainty, fear, or distress often accompanying thoughts and feelings about gender. Anxiegender individuals may find that their anxiety influences how they perceive and express their gender, leading to complex and multifaceted experiences.

Common Experiences and Challenges:
One common experience for individuals with anxiegender identity is the challenge of navigating the intersection of anxiety and gender identity. Anxiegender individuals may experience heightened levels of anxiety surrounding their gender, leading to feelings of discomfort, dysphoria, or distress as they grapple with their sense of self.

Anxiegender individuals may also face challenges in accessing support and resources to address their unique needs. The close connection between anxiety and gender identity may require specialized care and understanding from mental health professionals and support networks, yet anxiegender individuals may struggle to find providers who are knowledgeable and affirming of their experiences.

Furthermore, anxiegender individuals may encounter difficulties in finding acceptance and validation for their identity, as it can be less recognized or understood compared to more mainstream gender identities. They may feel misunderstood or invalidated by others who fail to recognize the impact of anxiety on their gender identity.

Despite these challenges, many anxiegender individuals find strength and resilience in acknowledging and affirming their unique identity. They may seek out supportive communities and resources that prioritize understanding and compassion for individuals navigating the complex intersection of anxiety and gender identity.

Illustrative Example:

Alex: Alex identifies as anxiegender and experiences their gender identity as deeply intertwined with feelings of anxiety. They struggle with persistent feelings of uncertainty and fear surrounding their gender, which can manifest in heightened levels of distress or dysphoria.

Despite these challenges, Alex finds empowerment and validation in acknowledging and affirming their anxiegender identity, seeking out support and resources that prioritize understanding and compassion for individuals navigating similar experiences.

Apagender: Apathetic or Lack of Feelings Toward Gender Identity

Definition and Characteristics:
Apagender is a gender identity characterized by apathy or a lack of strong feelings toward one's gender identity. Individuals who identify as apagender may experience a sense of detachment or indifference when it comes to their gender, lacking strong emotional connections or attachments to any particular gender identity. The term "apagender" emphasizes the absence of strong feelings or emotional investment in one's gender identity.

Characteristics of apagender may include a sense of neutrality or ambivalence regarding gender, with individuals feeling neither strongly connected nor disconnected from any particular gender identity. Apagender individuals may find that their gender identity is less salient or central to their sense of self compared to other aspects of their identity.

Common Experiences and Challenges:
One common experience for individuals with apagender identity is the challenge of navigating a world that often emphasizes the importance of gender identity in shaping one's sense of self and social interactions. Apagender individuals may feel pressure to conform to societal expectations or norms regarding gender, leading to feelings of discomfort or dissonance as they grapple with their lack of strong feelings toward their gender identity.

Apagender individuals may also encounter difficulties in finding acceptance and validation for their identity, as it can be less recognized or understood compared to more mainstream gender identities. They may feel misunderstood or invalidated by others who struggle to comprehend the concept of a lack of emotional attachment to one's gender identity.

Furthermore, apagender individuals may experience challenges in accessing supportive resources or communities that fully embrace and understand the complexity of their gender identity. They may feel disconnected or marginalized within both LGBTQ+ and cisgender communities, leading to feelings of isolation or invisibility.

Despite these challenges, many apagender individuals find empowerment and validation in embracing their unique identity and advocating for greater acceptance and understanding of diverse gender experiences within broader society.

Illustrative Example:

Jordan: Jordan identifies as apagender and experiences a sense of detachment or indifference toward their gender identity. They feel neither strongly connected nor disconnected from any particular gender identity, leading to feelings of neutrality or ambivalence regarding gender. Despite facing challenges in navigating societal expectations and norms, Jordan finds strength and resilience in asserting their authentic self and advocating for greater acceptance and understanding of diverse gender experiences.

Apconsugender: Awareness of What Gender Is Not, But Uncertainty About Its Characteristics

Definition and Characteristics:
Apconsugender describes a gender identity where an individual has a clear understanding of what characteristics do not align with their gender identity, but they are uncertain or unable to identify what specific characteristics define their gender. In essence, individuals who identify as apconsugender are aware of what aspects of gender do not resonate with them, but they struggle to pinpoint or articulate what exactly does define their gender identity. The term "apconsugender" underscores the sense of ambiguity and uncertainty surrounding one's gender identity.

Characteristics of apconsugender may include a sense of confusion or ambiguity regarding one's gender identity, with individuals feeling a disconnect from certain gendered traits or roles while simultaneously lacking a clear understanding of what aspects do align with their gender. Apconsugender individuals may experience a sense of frustration or discomfort as they navigate the complexity of their gender identity.

Common Experiences and Challenges:
One common experience for individuals with apconsugender identity is the challenge of navigating a world that often expects individuals to neatly fit into predefined gender categories.

Apconsugender individuals may struggle with feelings of confusion or frustration as they grapple with the uncertainty surrounding their gender identity, particularly when faced with societal pressure to conform to traditional gender norms or expectations.

Apconsugender individuals may also encounter difficulties in finding acceptance and validation for their identity, as it can be less recognized or understood compared to more mainstream gender identities. They may feel misunderstood or invalidated by others who struggle to comprehend the complexity of their experiences.

Furthermore, apconsugender individuals may experience challenges in accessing supportive resources or communities that fully embrace and understand the ambiguity and uncertainty of their gender identity. They may feel isolated or marginalized within both LGBTQ+ and cisgender communities, leading to feelings of invisibility or invalidation.

Despite these challenges, many apconsugender individuals find strength and resilience in embracing the complexity of their gender identity and advocating for greater acceptance and understanding of diverse gender experiences within broader society.

Illustrative Example:

Alex: Alex identifies as apconsugender and experiences a sense of confusion and uncertainty surrounding their gender identity.

They are acutely aware of what aspects of gender do not align with them, but they struggle to identify or articulate what specific characteristics do define their gender. Despite facing challenges in navigating societal expectations and norms, Alex finds strength and resilience in asserting their authentic self and advocating for greater acceptance and understanding of diverse gender experiences.

Astergender individuals often describe their gender as being intimately connected to the celestial realm, feeling a profound alignment with the majesty of the universe. Like stars scattered across the night sky, their gender identity glimmers with a celestial luminescence, casting a radiant glow upon their sense of self. For them, gender is not confined by earthly boundaries but instead reaches beyond, encompassing the vastness of space and the infinite possibilities it holds.

However, traversing the cosmos of gender identity is not without its challenges. Astergender individuals may find themselves navigating a universe that often fails to comprehend or accommodate their unique experience. In a world bound by binary notions of gender, they may encounter skepticism or misunderstanding from those who struggle to perceive the luminous intricacies of astergender identity. Finding validation and acceptance amidst a society that gravitates towards simplicity can be akin to searching for a single star in a vast galaxy.

Yet, despite these challenges, astergender individuals continue to shine brightly, illuminating the path towards greater understanding and inclusivity.

Through their resilience and self-expression, they invite others to gaze upon the brilliance of their gender identity and marvel at the wonders of the cosmos within.

To better understand astergender, consider the story of Alex, whose gender identity sparkles like a constellation in the night sky. From a young age, Alex felt a profound connection to the stars, finding solace and affirmation in the vastness of space. They would spend countless nights gazing up at the heavens, feeling as though each twinkling star whispered secrets of their truest self.

As they grew older, Alex came to realize that their gender was as boundless and luminous as the universe itself. They embraced the term "astergender" as a beacon of their identity, finding comfort in the celestial metaphor it provided. Though they faced skepticism and confusion from some, Alex remained steadfast in their self-understanding, knowing that their gender was as real and radiant as the stars that adorned the night sky.

Through their journey, Alex serves as a reminder that gender, like the cosmos, is vast, diverse, and infinitely beautiful. In embracing the brilliance of their astergender identity, they invite others to look beyond the confines of earthly labels and behold the awe-inspiring complexity of the gender galaxy.

Embark on a cosmic journey through the realm of gender identity, where the stars themselves whisper secrets of self-discovery. **Astral gender**, much like the boundless expanse of space, beckons individuals to explore the depths of their inner universe, where their gender identity aligns with the celestial wonders above. Picture a sense of self that orbits the cosmos, tethered to the constellations and nebulae that adorn the night sky, guiding one's understanding of who they are in a vast and wondrous universe.

At its core, astral gender encompasses a deep-seated connection to the mysteries of space, where one's gender identity resonates with the cosmic energies that permeate the universe. Individuals who identify as astral gender often describe a profound sense of kinship with celestial bodies, feeling as though their gender is intricately woven into the fabric of the cosmos. Like stars adrift in the infinite expanse, their gender identity radiates with a luminous intensity, casting a celestial glow upon their sense of self.

However, navigating the cosmic landscape of gender identity is not without its challenges. Astral gender individuals may find themselves grappling with a sense of isolation or alienation, as they seek validation and understanding in a world that often struggles to comprehend the intricacies of their experience. In a society bound by earthly norms and conventions, they may face skepticism or disbelief from those who fail to grasp the ethereal nature of astral gender identity.

Yet, amidst the challenges, there exists a sense of wonder and possibility. Astral gender individuals are pioneers of self-discovery, charting unexplored territories of gender identity with courage and resilience. Through their journey, they illuminate the cosmos of gender diversity, inviting others to gaze upon the beauty and complexity of the universe within.

To grasp the essence of astral gender, consider the story of Maya, whose gender identity soars among the stars like a comet streaking across the night sky. From a young age, Maya felt a magnetic pull towards the cosmos, finding solace and inspiration in the twinkling lights above. They would spend hours immersed in books about astronomy, feeling as though each page held the key to unlocking the mysteries of their own identity.

As they grew older, Maya came to realize that their gender was as vast and boundless as the universe itself. They embraced the term "astral gender" as a testament to their celestial connection, finding solace in the knowledge that their identity was as expansive as the cosmos. Though they faced challenges along the way, Maya remained steadfast in their truth, knowing that their gender identity was as real and immutable as the stars that adorned the night sky.

Through their journey, Maya serves as a beacon of light in the vast expanse of gender diversity, reminding us all to look beyond the confines of earthly labels and embrace the infinite possibilities of the cosmos within.

Dive into the intricate tapestry of identity, where the threads of autism and gender weave together to form the unique fabric of **autigender**. This gender identity, akin to a finely tuned symphony, harmonizes with the nuanced experiences of being autistic, creating a profound sense of self that resonates with the complexities of neurodiversity. Imagine a gender identity that unfolds like the pages of a novel, revealing layers of insight and understanding rooted in the rich terrain of autism spectrum.

At its essence, autigender embodies a deeply intertwined relationship between gender and autism, where one's sense of self is intricately shaped by their neurodivergent experiences. Individuals who identify as autigender often describe a profound alignment between their gender identity and the cognitive, sensory, and social aspects of being autistic. Like a kaleidoscope of colors, their gender identity is vibrant and multifaceted, reflecting the unique patterns of their autistic experience.

Yet, navigating the intersection of autism and gender identity is not without its challenges. Autigender individuals may find themselves grappling with a myriad of complex emotions and societal expectations, as they navigate the often turbulent waters of self-discovery. In a world that often struggles to understand the intricacies of autism spectrum, they may face skepticism or disbelief from those who fail to recognize the profound connection between their neurodivergent identity and their gender.

However, amidst the challenges, there exists a sense of resilience and authenticity. Autigender individuals are pioneers of self-expression, forging pathways of understanding and acceptance in a world that too often seeks conformity. Through their journey, they invite others to embrace the beauty and complexity of neurodiversity, celebrating the rich tapestry of human experience.

To illuminate the essence of autigender, consider the story of Sam, whose gender identity unfolds like a map of constellations, each star a testament to their autistic experience. From a young age, Sam navigated the world with a unique perspective, finding solace and comfort in the familiar rhythms of routine and sensory exploration. They would spend hours lost in their own world, finding joy in the intricate details of their special interests.

As they grew older, Sam came to realize that their gender identity was as complex and nuanced as their experience of autism. They embraced the term "autigender" as a reflection of their deeply intertwined identity, finding solace in the knowledge that their gender was an integral part of their neurodivergent journey. Though they faced challenges along the way, Sam remained steadfast in their truth, knowing that their gender identity was as real and valid as the vibrant spectrum of their autistic experience.

Through their journey, Sam serves as a beacon of hope and understanding in the vast landscape of neurodiversity, reminding us all to embrace the richness of human variation and celebrate the beauty of being authentically ourselves.

Delve into the intimate depths of self-discovery, where the essence of gender blooms uniquely within each individual like a rare and precious flower. Autogender, a term that echoes with the resonance of selfhood, embodies a gender experience that is deeply personal and profoundly connected to one's innermost being. Imagine a gender identity that unfurls like the petals of a blossoming rose, rooted in the fertile soil of self-awareness and introspection.

At its core, autogender encapsulates the profound intimacy between self and gender, where one's sense of identity is intricately woven into the fabric of their being. Individuals who identify as autogender often describe a deep sense of resonance and authenticity with their gender, recognizing it as a fundamental aspect of their identity that is uniquely their own. Like a symphony composed of the soul's most intimate melodies, their gender identity resonates with a profound sense of belonging and self-understanding.

Yet, traversing the terrain of autogender is not without its challenges. Autogender individuals may grapple with a myriad of complex emotions and societal expectations as they navigate the landscape of self-discovery. In a world that often seeks to impose rigid categories and labels, they may face skepticism or misunderstanding from those who struggle to comprehend the deeply personal nature of their gender experience.

However, amidst the challenges, there exists a sense of empowerment and liberation. Autogender individuals are pioneers of self-expression, forging pathways of authenticity and self-acceptance in a world that too often seeks conformity. Through their journey, they invite others to embrace the beauty and complexity of individuality, celebrating the rich tapestry of human experience.

To illuminate the essence of autogender, consider the story of Jamie, whose gender identity blossoms like a garden in full bloom, each petal a testament to their unique journey of self-discovery. From a young age, Jamie felt a profound sense of alignment with their gender, recognizing it as an intrinsic part of their being that could not be defined by external expectations or societal norms. They embraced the term "autogender" as a reflection of their deeply personal experience, finding solace in the knowledge that their gender was an expression of their truest self.

As they grew older, Jamie embarked on a journey of self-exploration and acceptance, embracing their autogender identity with courage and conviction. Though they faced challenges along the way, Jamie remained steadfast in their truth, knowing that their gender identity was as real and valid as the beating of their own heart.

Through their journey, Jamie serves as a beacon of authenticity and empowerment, reminding us all to embrace the beauty of self-discovery and celebrate the richness of our individuality.

Step into the liminal space where gender intersects with the spectrum of identity, and you'll find **axigender**—a nuanced and dynamic gender experience that navigates the delicate balance between agender and another gender along a distinct axis. Imagine standing at the crossroads where the essence of gender unfolds along a continuum, with agender at one pole and another gender at the opposite end, each experienced separately without overlap. Picture this axis as a bridge between two distinct realms of identity, where individuals traverse the space between with grace and introspection.

At its essence, axigender embodies the interplay between absence and presence, as individuals navigate the terrain between agender and another gender with clarity and self-awareness. Those who identify as axigender often describe experiencing each gender distinctly, one at a time, without blending or merging of identities. Like a delicate dance along the tightrope of self-discovery, their gender experience is characterized by a keen awareness of the nuanced shifts between agender and their other gender.

However, navigating the delicate balance of axigender is not without its challenges. Individuals may grapple with questions of identity and self-understanding as they navigate the space between agender and their other gender. In a society that often seeks to categorize and label, they may face skepticism or misunderstanding from those who struggle to comprehend the fluidity and complexity of their gender experience.

Yet, amidst the challenges, there exists a sense of empowerment and authenticity. Axigender individuals are pioneers of self-expression, forging pathways of understanding and acceptance in a world that too often seeks conformity. Through their journey, they invite others to embrace the beauty and complexity of gender diversity, celebrating the richness of human experience along the spectrum of identity.

To illuminate the essence of axigender, consider the story of Taylor, whose gender identity unfolds like a delicate balancing act between two distinct poles. From a young age, Taylor grappled with questions of identity, feeling a profound sense of resonance with both agender and another gender. They embraced the term "axigender" as a reflection of their fluid and nuanced experience, finding solace in the knowledge that their identity defied rigid categorization.

As they grew older, Taylor embarked on a journey of self-discovery and self-acceptance, navigating the space between agender and their other gender with courage and conviction. Though they faced challenges along the way, Taylor remained steadfast in their truth, knowing that their gender identity was as real and valid as the intricate dance of stars in the night sky.

Through their journey, Taylor serves as a beacon of authenticity and empowerment, reminding us all to embrace the beauty of fluidity and celebrate the richness of our diverse identities along the spectrum of gender.

Enter the realm of gender multiplicity, where the experience of self is not confined to a single identity but expands to encompass the duality of bigender. Bigender individuals navigate the intricate landscape of gender with a sense of fluidity and versatility, embodying two distinct gender identities either simultaneously or at different times. Imagine the weaving together of two vibrant threads of identity, each contributing to the rich tapestry of self-expression and self-understanding.

At its core, **bigender** embodies the dynamic interplay between two gender identities, allowing individuals to inhabit multiple gender expressions with authenticity and clarity. Common characteristics include experiencing a sense of alignment with both masculine and feminine genders, whether simultaneously or shifting between them over time. Like a kaleidoscope of colors, their gender identity is multifaceted and ever-changing, reflecting the complexity of human experience.

However, navigating the terrain of bigender is not without its challenges. Individuals may grapple with questions of identity and self-acceptance as they navigate the delicate balance between two genders. In a society that often seeks to impose rigid binary norms, bigender individuals may face skepticism or misunderstanding from those who struggle to comprehend the fluidity and complexity of their gender experience.

Yet, amidst the challenges, there exists a sense of empowerment and authenticity. Bigender individuals are pioneers of self-expression, forging pathways of understanding and acceptance in a world that too often seeks conformity.

Through their journey, they invite others to embrace the beauty of gender diversity, celebrating the richness of human experience along the spectrum of identity.

To illuminate the essence of bigender, consider the story of Alex, whose gender identity unfolds like a dance between two partners, each step a testament to their unique journey of self-discovery. From a young age, Alex grappled with questions of identity, feeling a deep resonance with both masculine and feminine genders. They embraced the term "bigender" as a reflection of their fluid and nuanced experience, finding solace in the knowledge that their identity defied rigid categorization.

As they grew older, Alex embraced their bigender identity with courage and conviction, navigating the terrain of gender with grace and authenticity. Though they faced challenges along the way, Alex remained steadfast in their truth, knowing that their gender identity was as real and valid as the intricate tapestry of their lived experience.

Through their journey, Alex serves as a beacon of authenticity and empowerment, reminding us all to embrace the beauty of fluidity and celebrate the richness of our diverse identities along the spectrum of gender.

Embark on a journey through the verdant landscapes of identity, where the essence of gender intertwines intimately with the rhythms of the natural world, giving rise to the concept of biogender. This gender identity, akin to the fertile soil from which life springs forth, is deeply rooted in the beauty and interconnectedness of nature. Imagine a gender experience that blooms like wildflowers in a meadow, shaped by the whispers of the wind, the murmur of streams, and the rustle of leaves.

At its essence, **biogender** encapsulates a profound sense of harmony and resonance with the natural world, where one's gender identity is intricately intertwined with the rhythms, energies, and forms found in nature. Individuals who identify as biogender often describe feeling a deep connection to the elements, flora, and fauna, recognizing their gender as an expression of the beauty and diversity of the world around them. Like the ebb and flow of the tide, their gender identity is fluid and ever-changing, shaped by the cycles of the earth and the seasons.

However, navigating the terrain of biogender is not without its challenges. Individuals may grapple with questions of identity and self-acceptance as they seek to understand the intricate interplay between their gender and the natural world. In a society that often seeks to separate humanity from nature, biogender individuals may face skepticism or misunderstanding from those who struggle to comprehend the depth of their connection to the earth.

Yet, amidst the challenges, there exists a sense of empowerment and authenticity.

Biogender individuals are stewards of the earth, forging pathways of understanding and reverence for the natural world in a world that too often seeks to exploit and dominate. Through their journey, they invite others to embrace the beauty and interconnectedness of nature, celebrating the richness of human experience as an integral part of the web of life.

To illuminate the essence of biogender, consider the story of Maya, whose gender identity unfurls like the branches of an ancient oak tree, rooted deeply in the soil of the earth. From a young age, Maya felt a profound sense of connection to nature, finding solace and inspiration in the beauty and diversity of the world around them. They embraced the term "biogender" as a reflection of their deep bond with the natural world, finding solace in the knowledge that their gender was an expression of the interconnectedness of all living things.

As they grew older, Maya embraced their biogender identity with courage and conviction, nurturing their connection to nature and celebrating the beauty of diversity in all its forms. Though they faced challenges along the way, Maya remained steadfast in their truth, knowing that their gender identity was as real and valid as the intricate web of life that surrounds us all.

Through their journey, Maya serves as a beacon of authenticity and empowerment, reminding us all to embrace the beauty of nature and celebrate the richness of our diverse identities as an integral part of the earth's tapestry.

Enter the realm of gender fluidity, where the boundaries between identities blur and merge like colors on an artist's palette, giving rise to the concept of blurgender. Also known as gender fuss, blurgender individuals experience a fluidity of gender identity where multiple genders intertwine and blend seamlessly, creating a unique and ever-changing landscape of self-expression. Imagine a gender identity that dances along the edges of perception, shifting and evolving with the ebb and flow of individual experience.

At its essence, **blurgender** encapsulates the dynamic interplay between multiple gender identities, where distinctions between them become hazy and indistinct. Common characteristics include a sense of fluidity and ambiguity, with individuals experiencing a spectrum of gender expressions that defy traditional categorization. Like a collage of shapes and colors, their gender identity is multifaceted and complex, reflecting the diverse and ever-changing nature of human experience.

However, navigating the terrain of blurgender is not without its challenges. Individuals may grapple with questions of identity and self-acceptance as they navigate the fluidity of their gender experience. In a society that often seeks clear-cut labels and categories, blurgender individuals may face skepticism or misunderstanding from those who struggle to comprehend the intricacies of their identity.

Yet, amidst the challenges, there exists a sense of liberation and authenticity.

Blurgender individuals are pioneers of self-expression, forging pathways of understanding and acceptance in a world that too often seeks conformity. Through their journey, they invite others to embrace the beauty of fluidity and celebrate the richness of human experience along the spectrum of gender.

To illustrate the essence of blurgender, consider the story of Sam, whose gender identity shimmers like a mirage in the desert, elusive yet captivating. From a young age, Sam grappled with questions of identity, feeling a sense of resonance with multiple gender expressions that seemed to blur and merge together. They embraced the term "blurgender" as a reflection of their fluid and ever-changing experience, finding solace in the knowledge that their identity defied rigid categorization.

As they grew older, Sam embraced their blurgender identity with courage and conviction, navigating the shifting sands of gender with grace and authenticity. Though they faced challenges along the way, Sam remained steadfast in their truth, knowing that their gender identity was as real and valid as the kaleidoscope of colors that danced in the desert sun.

Through their journey, Sam serves as a beacon of authenticity and empowerment, reminding us all to embrace the beauty of fluidity and celebrate the richness of our diverse identities along the spectrum of gender.

Step into the nuanced realm of gender fluctuation, where the experience of masculinity unfolds along a dynamic spectrum, giving rise to the concept of boyflux. Individuals who identify as boyflux experience shifts in their sense of male identity, fluctuating between varying degrees of masculinity, ranging from feeling agender to fully embracing their male identity. Imagine a gender identity that ebbs and flows like the tides, with moments of clarity and resonance followed by periods of ambiguity and fluidity.

At its core, boyflux embodies the fluidity and variability of gender identity, where individuals experience a dynamic interplay between different degrees of male identification. Common characteristics include moments of feeling strongly aligned with masculinity, followed by periods of feeling more agender or gender-neutral. Like a pendulum swinging between poles, their gender identity is characterized by a constant state of flux and evolution, reflecting the ever-changing nature of self-perception.

However, navigating the terrain of boyflux is not without its challenges. Individuals may grapple with questions of identity and self-acceptance as they navigate the fluctuations of their gender experience. In a society that often seeks clear-cut labels and categories, boyflux individuals may face skepticism or misunderstanding from those who struggle to comprehend the complexity of their identity.

Yet, amidst the challenges, there exists a sense of resilience and authenticity.

Boyflux individuals are pioneers of self-discovery, forging pathways of understanding and acceptance in a world that too often seeks conformity. Through their journey, they invite others to embrace the beauty of fluidity and celebrate the richness of human experience along the spectrum of gender.

To illustrate the essence of boyflux, consider the story of Alex, whose gender identity unfolds like a kaleidoscope of colors, shifting and changing with each turn of the wheel. From a young age, Alex grappled with questions of identity, feeling a sense of resonance with masculinity but also experiencing moments of gender ambiguity and neutrality. They embraced the term "boyflux" as a reflection of their fluid and ever-changing experience, finding solace in the knowledge that their identity defied rigid categorization.

As they grew older, Alex embraced their boyflux identity with courage and conviction, navigating the fluctuations of gender with grace and authenticity. Though they faced challenges along the way, Alex remained steadfast in their truth, knowing that their gender identity was as real and valid as the shifting sands of time.

Through their journey, Alex serves as a beacon of authenticity and empowerment, reminding us all to embrace the beauty of fluidity and celebrate the richness of our diverse identities along the spectrum of gender.

In the ever-evolving landscape of gender identity, **burstgender** emerges as a dynamic and vivid experience characterized by frequent bursts of intense feelings followed by a return to a state of calm. Imagine a gender identity that flickers like a flame, erupting with intensity before settling back into a tranquil state, only to burst forth again with renewed vigor. Burstgender individuals navigate the peaks and valleys of their gender experience with a sense of fluidity and resilience, embracing the intensity of their emotions while finding solace in moments of peace and stability.

At its core, burstgender embodies the cyclical nature of emotional expression, where individuals experience intense bursts of gender feelings that quickly dissipate, returning them to a state of equilibrium. Common characteristics include moments of heightened intensity, marked by a surge of gender affirmation or dysphoria, followed by a period of calm and reflection. Like a storm rolling across the sky, their gender identity is characterized by moments of turbulence and calm, each contributing to the rich tapestry of their lived experience.

However, navigating the terrain of burstgender is not without its challenges. Individuals may grapple with the intense fluctuations of their gender experience, struggling to find stability amidst the storm of emotions. In a society that often seeks clear-cut labels and categories, burstgender individuals may face skepticism or misunderstanding from those who struggle to comprehend the complexity of their identity.

Yet, amidst the challenges, there exists a sense of resilience and authenticity.

Burstgender individuals are pioneers of self-expression, embracing the intensity of their emotions while finding strength in moments of calm and reflection. Through their journey, they invite others to embrace the beauty of fluidity and celebrate the richness of human experience along the spectrum of gender.

To illustrate the essence of burstgender, consider the story of Taylor, whose gender identity unfolds like a series of waves crashing upon the shore, each one more intense than the last. From a young age, Taylor grappled with questions of identity, experiencing intense bursts of gender feelings that would quickly dissipate, leaving them feeling adrift in a sea of uncertainty. They embraced the term "burstgender" as a reflection of their dynamic and ever-changing experience, finding solace in the knowledge that their identity defied rigid categorization.

As they grew older, Taylor learned to embrace the intensity of their gender experience, finding strength in moments of calm and reflection. Though they faced challenges along the way, Taylor remained steadfast in their truth, knowing that their gender identity was as real and valid as the shifting tides of the ocean.

Through their journey, Taylor serves as a beacon of authenticity and empowerment, reminding us all to embrace the beauty of fluidity and celebrate the richness of our diverse identities along the spectrum of gender.

In the vast expanse of gender identity, there exists a celestial phenomenon known as **caelgender**, where the essence of one's gender is imbued with the qualities and aesthetics of outer space. Imagine a gender identity that shimmers with the iridescence of distant galaxies, echoing the vastness and beauty of the cosmos. Caelgender individuals navigate the cosmos of their own identity with a sense of wonder and awe, finding resonance in the celestial wonders that adorn the night sky.

At its core, caelgender embodies a deep connection to the majesty of outer space, where one's gender identity is shaped by the ethereal qualities and aesthetics of the cosmos. Common characteristics include a sense of expansiveness and boundlessness, as well as an affinity for celestial imagery and symbolism. Like stars scattered across the velvet expanse of space, their gender identity twinkles with a luminous brilliance, casting a radiant glow upon their sense of self.

However, navigating the terrain of caelgender is not without its challenges. Individuals may grapple with questions of identity and self-expression as they seek to articulate the ineffable qualities of their gender experience. In a society that often seeks clear-cut labels and categories, caelgender individuals may face skepticism or misunderstanding from those who struggle to comprehend the cosmic dimensions of their identity.

Yet, amidst the challenges, there exists a sense of wonder and possibility.

Caelgender individuals are pioneers of self-expression, forging pathways of understanding and acceptance in a world that too often seeks conformity. Through their journey, they invite others to gaze upon the beauty and complexity of the universe within, celebrating the vastness and diversity of human experience along the spectrum of gender.

To illustrate the essence of caelgender, consider the story of Alex, whose gender identity unfolds like a constellation in the night sky, each star a testament to their cosmic connection. From a young age, Alex felt a profound sense of awe and wonder when gazing up at the stars, finding solace and inspiration in the mysteries of the cosmos. They embraced the term "caelgender" as a reflection of their celestial identity, finding solace in the knowledge that their gender was as boundless and infinite as the universe itself.

As they grew older, Alex learned to embrace the cosmic dimensions of their identity, finding strength and empowerment in their connection to the stars. Though they faced challenges along the way, Alex remained steadfast in their truth, knowing that their gender identity was as real and valid as the shimmering expanse of space that stretches out before us.

Within the realm of gender identity lies the tranquil landscape of **cassgender**, a serene state where the concept of gender holds little to no significance. Cassgender individuals experience a sense of detachment or indifference towards gender, viewing it as irrelevant or unimportant to their sense of self. Imagine a gender identity that is as calm and peaceful as a quiet stream, flowing gently through the landscape of the mind without the tumultuous waves of gender-related expectations or pressures.

At its essence, cassgender embodies a profound sense of liberation from societal constructs and expectations surrounding gender. Common characteristics include a feeling of neutrality or apathy towards gender labels, as well as a sense of freedom from the constraints of traditional gender roles. Like a tranquil lake reflecting the sky above, their gender identity is serene and reflective, mirroring the inner landscape of their truest self.

However, navigating the terrain of cassgender is not without its challenges. Individuals may grapple with questions of identity and self-expression as they seek to articulate the subtleties of their gender experience. In a society that often places great emphasis on gender identity and expression, cassgender individuals may face skepticism or misunderstanding from those who struggle to comprehend the depth of their indifference towards gender.

Yet, amidst the challenges, there exists a sense of peace and authenticity.

Cassgender individuals are pioneers of self-acceptance, forging pathways of understanding and empowerment in a world that too often seeks to categorize and label. Through their journey, they invite others to embrace the beauty of self-determination and celebrate the richness of human experience beyond the confines of gender.

To illustrate the essence of cassgender, consider the story of Taylor, whose gender identity unfolds like a tranquil meadow, bathed in the soft glow of the setting sun. From a young age, Taylor felt a sense of detachment from societal expectations surrounding gender, viewing it as a superficial and irrelevant aspect of their identity. They embraced the term "cassgender" as a reflection of their serene indifference towards gender, finding solace in the knowledge that their identity was defined by their own sense of self rather than external labels or expectations.

As they grew older, Taylor learned to embrace their cassgender identity with grace and confidence, finding strength in their sense of liberation from societal norms. Though they faced challenges along the way, Taylor remained steadfast in their truth, knowing that their gender identity was as valid and real as the tranquil landscape that lay within.

Through their journey, Taylor serves as a beacon of authenticity and empowerment, reminding us all to embrace the beauty of self-acceptance and celebrate the richness of human diversity beyond the confines of gender.

The concept of **cassflux** introduces a dynamic and ever-shifting landscape where the intensity of indifference towards gender fluctuates over time. Cassflux individuals experience varying degrees of detachment or irrelevance towards gender, with the intensity of these feelings ebbing and flowing like the tides. Imagine a gender identity that is as changeable and fluid as a river, with moments of deep indifference followed by periods of heightened awareness or significance.

At its core, cassflux embodies the nuanced interplay between indifference towards gender and moments of heightened awareness or significance. Common characteristics include experiencing fluctuations in the intensity of feelings towards gender, with periods of apathy or neutrality followed by times of increased awareness or engagement. Like a river carving its path through the landscape, their gender identity is shaped by the ever-changing currents of their inner experience.

However, navigating the terrain of cassflux is not without its challenges. Individuals may grapple with questions of identity and self-understanding as they navigate the fluctuations of their gender experience. In a society that often seeks clear-cut labels and categories, cassflux individuals may face skepticism or misunderstanding from those who struggle to comprehend the complexity of their identity.

Yet, amidst the challenges, there exists a sense of authenticity and self-awareness. Cassflux individuals are pioneers of self-exploration, embracing the fluidity of their gender experience and finding strength in their ability to navigate the shifting currents of their inner landscape. Through their journey, they invite others to embrace the beauty of complexity and celebrate the richness of human experience along the spectrum of gender.

To illustrate the essence of cassflux, consider the story of Alex, whose gender identity flows like a river, with moments of calm followed by turbulent rapids. From a young age, Alex experienced fluctuations in their feelings towards gender, with periods of deep indifference interspersed with moments of heightened awareness or significance. They embraced the term "cassflux" as a reflection of their ever-changing experience, finding solace in the knowledge that their gender identity was as dynamic and fluid as the river that flowed through their soul.

Cavusgender illuminates a unique intersection between mood and gender identity, where an individual's sense of gender fluctuates in tandem with their emotional state. Specifically, cavusgender individuals feel a closer connection to one gender when experiencing depression, while aligning more closely with another gender when not depressed.

Common experiences associated with cavusgender include a profound awareness of the influence of mood on one's gender identity, with shifts occurring in response to changes in emotional well-being. These shifts may manifest as changes in self-perception, feelings of alignment with different gender expressions, or shifts in preferred pronouns.

Challenges faced by cavusgender individuals often revolve around navigating the complexities of their gender identity within the context of mental health. These challenges may include:

Identity Fluidity: Managing the fluctuating nature of gender identity can lead to uncertainty and confusion about one's sense of self, particularly during periods of depression or mood instability.

Social Validation: Seeking validation and understanding from others regarding the validity of their gender identity, especially when it shifts in response to changes in mood.

Navigating Mental Health Support: Finding mental health professionals who are knowledgeable and supportive of both gender identity and mood-related concerns can be challenging.

Self-Acceptance: Striving to accept and embrace the dynamic nature of one's gender identity, recognizing that it is valid and deserving of affirmation regardless of mood fluctuations.

Overall, cavusgender individuals navigate a complex interplay between mood and gender identity, seeking to understand and honor their shifting sense of self while managing the challenges that arise along the way. Through self-awareness, self-acceptance, and supportive communities, they strive to find stability and empowerment within their unique journey of identity exploration.

Cendgender encapsulates a profound journey of gender fluidity, where individuals experience a shifting and dynamic spectrum of gender identity that oscillates between one gender and its opposite. Imagine a gender identity that is in constant motion, flowing like a river between two distinct poles, each representing a different gender expression. Cendgender individuals navigate this fluidity with a sense of self-awareness and acceptance, embracing the ever-changing nature of their gender experience.

Common experiences associated with cendgender include a deep sense of flux and transformation, where individuals may feel a strong alignment with one gender identity at one moment, only to transition to its opposite at another. These shifts in gender identity may occur gradually or suddenly, leading to a profound sense of fluidity and uncertainty about one's sense of self.

Challenges faced by cendgender individuals often revolve around navigating the complexities of identity within a society that often seeks clear-cut labels and categories. These challenges may include:

Identity Exploration: Continuously exploring and understanding one's gender identity as it fluctuates between two distinct poles, embracing the complexity of the journey.

Social Acceptance: Seeking acceptance and validation from others for the validity of their gender identity, especially in environments where gender fluidity is not well understood or accepted.

Navigating Relationships: Communicating with partners, friends, and family members about the fluid nature of their gender identity and how it may impact their relationships and interactions.

Internal Acceptance: Striving to accept and embrace the fluidity of one's gender identity, recognizing that it is valid and deserving of affirmation regardless of societal norms or expectations.

To illustrate the essence of cendgender, consider the story of Jordan, whose gender identity flows like a pendulum swinging between two opposing poles. From a young age, Jordan felt a deep sense of internal conflict, oscillating between moments of feeling strongly aligned with one gender and then shifting suddenly to its opposite. They embraced the term "cendgender" as a reflection of their fluid and ever-changing experience, finding solace in the knowledge that their gender identity was as dynamic and multifaceted as the shifting sands of time.

Ceterogender represents a unique nonbinary identity where individuals experience specific feelings of masculinity, femininity, or neutrality within their gender identity. Unlike binary genders, ceterogender encompasses a nuanced blend of gender expressions, allowing individuals to navigate their identity along a spectrum that incorporates elements of masculinity, femininity, and neutrality.

Common experiences associated with ceterogender include:

Fluidity of Expression: Ceterogender individuals may experience shifts in their gender expression, moving between feelings of masculinity, femininity, and neutrality depending on their mood, environment, or personal preferences.

Identity Exploration: Exploring and understanding the diverse facets of their gender identity, embracing the complexity of their experiences and how they intersect with different aspects of gender expression.

Validation and Acceptance: Seeking validation and acceptance from others for the validity of their nonbinary identity, especially in environments where gender diversity is not well understood or accepted.

Community Connection: Finding support and connection within nonbinary and gender-diverse communities, where individuals can share experiences, insights, and resources related to navigating ceterogender identity.

Challenges faced by ceterogender individuals may include:

Navigating Gendered Spaces: Negotiating gendered spaces such as restrooms, clothing stores, or social gatherings where expectations may be based on binary gender categories, leading to feelings of discomfort or exclusion.

Social Perception: Dealing with societal misconceptions or stereotypes about nonbinary identities, including pressure to conform to binary gender norms or expectations.

Healthcare Access: Accessing healthcare services that are inclusive and affirming of nonbinary identities, including finding healthcare providers who understand the unique needs and experiences of ceterogender individuals.

Legal Recognition: Advocating for legal recognition and protection of nonbinary identities, including updating identification documents, navigating legal processes, and challenging discriminatory policies or practices.

To illustrate the essence of ceterogender, consider the story of Taylor, whose gender identity unfolds like a tapestry woven from threads of masculinity, femininity, and neutrality. From a young age, Taylor felt a deep sense of connection to multiple aspects of gender expression, embracing the fluidity and complexity of their identity. They embraced the term "ceterogender" as a reflection of their multifaceted experience, finding solace in the knowledge that their gender identity was as diverse and nuanced as the spectrum of human expression.

Ceterofluid individuals navigate the intricate landscape of gender identity with a unique and dynamic experience, where their ceterogender identity fluctuates and evolves between different genders over time. Unlike static identities, ceterofluidity embodies a fluidity of gender expression that transcends fixed categories, allowing individuals to explore and embrace the diversity of their gender identity along a constantly shifting spectrum.

Common experiences associated with ceterofluidity include:

Fluctuations in Gender Expression: Ceterofluid individuals may experience frequent shifts in their gender expression, moving fluidly between different genders or gender combinations based on internal feelings, external influences, or situational factors.

Identity Exploration: Continuously exploring and understanding the nuances of their gender identity as it evolves and fluctuates over time, embracing the complexity of their experiences and how they intersect with different aspects of gender expression.

Navigating Fluidity: Developing coping strategies and self-care practices to navigate the fluidity of their gender identity, including maintaining a sense of stability and self-awareness amidst changing feelings and expressions.

Community Connection: Seeking support and connection within gender-diverse communities, where individuals can share experiences, insights, and resources related to navigating ceterofluid identity and finding validation and affirmation in their diverse gender expressions.

Challenges faced by ceterofluid individuals may include:

Identity Stability: Struggling with feelings of uncertainty or instability regarding their gender identity, especially in environments where static or binary identities are more commonly understood and accepted.

Social Perception: Dealing with societal misconceptions or stereotypes about gender fluidity, including pressure to conform to binary gender norms or expectations and facing discrimination or invalidation based on their fluid identity.

Navigating Relationships: Communicating with partners, friends, and family members about the fluid nature of their gender identity and how it may impact their relationships and interactions, including navigating changes in pronouns or gender expression over time.

Legal Recognition: Advocating for legal recognition and protection of fluid identities, including updating identification documents, navigating legal processes, and challenging discriminatory policies or practices that fail to recognize the validity of ceterofluid identity.

To illustrate the essence of ceterofluidity, consider the story of Alex, whose gender identity flows like a river, with ever-changing currents that shift between different genders and gender expressions. From a young age, Alex felt a deep sense of fluidity within their gender identity, embracing the diversity and complexity of their experiences as they evolved over time.

They embraced the term "ceterofluid" as a reflection of their dynamic and ever-changing identity, finding solace in the knowledge that their gender expression was as diverse and multifaceted as the spectrum of human experience.

Cisgender individuals experience a sense of alignment between the gender they were assigned at birth and their personal sense of gender identity throughout their lives. This alignment typically remains consistent and stable, with cisgender individuals feeling comfortable and at ease with the gender roles, expectations, and characteristics associated with their assigned gender. Common experiences for cisgender individuals include a sense of congruence between their physical body and their internal sense of gender, as well as a feeling of belonging within societal norms and expectations related to gender identity. Challenges faced by cisgender individuals may include navigating discussions and interactions with individuals who have different gender identities, as well as confronting societal pressures and stereotypes associated with traditional gender roles. To illustrate cisgender identity, consider the story of Emily, who was assigned female at birth and has always felt a deep sense of alignment with her female gender identity. Throughout her life, Emily has felt comfortable expressing herself within the expectations and roles associated with being a woman, finding fulfillment and acceptance within her identity as a cisgender individual.

Cloudgender is a gender identity that exists within the complex landscape of depersonalization and derealization disorder, where individuals experience a profound sense of detachment from their own gender identity, making it difficult or impossible to comprehend or understand. Within this state, the individual's gender feels obscured or obscured by a fog-like sensation, rendering it inaccessible or incomprehensible. Common experiences for cloudgender individuals include a pervasive sense of disconnection from their own sense of self, including their gender identity, as well as feelings of confusion, frustration, and isolation due to the inability to grasp or articulate their gender. Challenges faced by cloudgender individuals may include navigating a sense of alienation or disconnect from their own identity, as well as difficulty accessing appropriate support and resources to address the underlying depersonalization and derealization disorder. To illustrate cloudgender identity, consider the story of Sam, who experiences frequent episodes of depersonalization and derealization, causing their gender identity to feel distant and inaccessible. Despite efforts to understand or define their gender, Sam finds themselves caught in a perpetual haze, unable to grasp or comprehend their own sense of self. Through therapy and support, Sam works to navigate the challenges of depersonalization and derealization disorder, finding solace in the knowledge that their experiences are valid and deserving of recognition and understanding.

Collgender individuals experience the coexistence of multiple genders within themselves simultaneously, creating a rich and complex tapestry of identity. Unlike traditional notions of gender, which often dictate a singular identity, collgender individuals navigate a dynamic and multifaceted landscape where various genders intersect and intertwine. Common experiences include a profound sense of fluidity and diversity within their gender identity, as well as an awareness of the complexity and nuance inherent in their lived experience.

Challenges faced by collgender individuals may include:

Identity Integration: Navigating the complexities of multiple genders coexisting within oneself, including reconciling conflicting feelings or expressions and integrating them into a cohesive sense of self.

Social Perception: Confronting societal misconceptions or stereotypes about gender identity, including pressure to conform to binary or monolithic understandings of gender.

Validation and Acceptance: Seeking validation and acceptance from others for the validity of their collgender identity, especially in environments where gender diversity is not well understood or accepted.

Navigating Spaces: Negotiating gendered spaces and interactions where traditional understandings of gender may not fully capture the complexity of their identity, leading to feelings of invisibility or exclusion.

To illustrate collgender identity, consider the story of Alex, who experiences the coexistence of multiple genders within themselves simultaneously. From a young age, Alex has felt a profound sense of fluidity and diversity within their gender identity, embracing the complexity and richness of their experience. They identify as collgender, recognizing and celebrating the mosaic of genders that make up their sense of self. Through self-discovery and self-acceptance, Alex learns to navigate the challenges of collgender identity with resilience and authenticity, finding strength in their ability to embrace the full spectrum of their gender expression. Though they may face obstacles along the way, Alex remains steadfast in their truth, knowing that their collgender identity is valid and deserving of affirmation and recognition. Through their journey, Alex serves as a beacon of authenticity and empowerment, reminding us all to embrace the beauty of diversity and celebrate the richness of our gender identities along the spectrum of human experience.

Colorgender is a unique gender identity category where individuals use colors to describe or define their gender identity. Instead of relying on traditional gender labels, individuals may associate their gender with specific colors that resonate with their sense of self. For example, someone may identify as "pink gender" or "black gender," using these colors as descriptors for their gender identity. This form of gender expression allows individuals to embrace the symbolism and emotional resonance of colors as a means of understanding and articulating their gender experience.

Common experiences among colorgender individuals include:

Personal Connection: Feeling a deep personal connection to specific colors that resonate with their gender identity, often based on associations with symbolism, aesthetics, or emotional significance.

Creative Expression: Using colors as a form of creative expression to communicate their gender identity to others, such as through clothing, accessories, or artwork.

Sense of Empowerment: Finding empowerment and authenticity in using colors to describe their gender identity, allowing for a personalized and nuanced understanding of self.

Challenges faced by colorgender individuals may include:

Understanding and Acceptance: Navigating societal expectations and misunderstandings surrounding nontraditional forms of gender expression, including misconceptions or lack of awareness about colorgender identities.

Visibility and Recognition: Seeking visibility and recognition for colorgender identities within gender-diverse communities and broader society, advocating for inclusion and affirmation of diverse forms of gender expression.

Navigating Gendered Spaces: Negotiating gendered spaces and interactions where traditional understandings of gender may not fully capture the complexity of colorgender identities, leading to feelings of invisibility or exclusion.

To illustrate colorgender identity, consider the story of Taylor, who identifies as "blue gender." For Taylor, the color blue represents feelings of calmness, serenity, and introspection, qualities that deeply resonate with their sense of gender identity. Through their choice to embrace "blue gender," Taylor finds a sense of empowerment and authenticity in expressing their gender identity in a way that feels true to their inner self.

Though they may encounter challenges in navigating societal expectations or misunderstandings, Taylor remains steadfast in their truth, knowing that their colorgender identity is valid and deserving of recognition and acceptance. Through their journey, Taylor serves as a reminder of the diversity and richness of gender expression, inviting others to explore and celebrate the unique ways in which colors can shape and define our sense of self.

Commogender individuals experience a unique journey of self-discovery where they recognize that they are not cisgender, yet continue to identify as such for a period of time. This identity encompasses a complex interplay between self-awareness, societal expectations, and personal exploration of gender. Common experiences among commogender individuals include a sense of confusion or uncertainty about their gender identity, as well as feelings of discomfort or disconnection from traditional cisgender labels. Despite recognizing a misalignment with cisgender identity, commogender individuals may grapple with internalized beliefs or external pressures that inhibit them from fully embracing a non-cisgender identity. This internal conflict can lead to a period of self-denial or suppression of true gender feelings, as individuals navigate the complexities of identity formation and societal norms.

Challenges faced by commogender individuals may include:

Self-Acceptance: Overcoming internalized beliefs and societal pressures to acknowledge and embrace their true gender identity, even if it diverges from cisnormative expectations.

Identity Exploration: Navigating a journey of self-discovery and exploration to understand and articulate their gender identity beyond the confines of cisgender norms.

Navigating Social Spaces: Negotiating gendered spaces and interactions where traditional understandings of gender may not fully capture the complexity of their identity, leading to feelings of confusion or invisibility.

Seeking Validation: Seeking validation and acceptance from others for the validity of their gender identity, especially in environments where gender diversity is not well understood or accepted.

To illustrate commogender identity, consider the story of Jamie, who spent many years identifying as cisgender despite feeling a persistent sense of unease with their assigned gender. Growing up in a society with rigid gender norms and expectations, Jamie struggled to reconcile their internal feelings with external perceptions of gender. It was only after years of introspection and self-exploration that Jamie came to understand and embrace their true gender identity as non-cisgender. Looking back on their journey, Jamie recognizes the challenges they faced in acknowledging and accepting their identity, but also celebrates the authenticity and freedom that comes with living as their true self. Through their experience, Jamie serves as a reminder of the complexity and fluidity of gender identity, inviting others to explore and embrace their own truths with courage and self-compassion.

Condigender individuals traverse the intricate terrain of gender identity with a unique twist, experiencing their gender only under specific circumstances. Picture a delicate flower that blooms only under the gentle touch of sunlight; similarly, condigender individuals find that their gender blossoms and reveals itself only in certain contexts or environments. This phenomenon imbues their gender identity with a sense of temporality and contextuality, where the full spectrum of their gender expression emerges and retreats like the ebb and flow of the tide.

Common experiences among condigender individuals include a heightened awareness of the factors or conditions that trigger their gender to manifest. Whether it's in the presence of certain people, during particular activities, or in specific settings, these circumstances serve as catalysts that awaken their sense of gender identity. For some, this may manifest as a sense of alignment and authenticity, while for others, it may evoke feelings of confusion or uncertainty as they navigate the ever-shifting landscape of their gender expression.

Challenges faced by condigender individuals often revolve around navigating the unpredictability and variability of their gender experience. The fleeting nature of their gender identity can lead to feelings of instability or inconsistency, making it difficult to maintain a sense of continuity or coherence in their sense of self. Additionally, condigender individuals may struggle with articulating or validating their gender identity to others, especially when it emerges only in specific circumstances that may not be readily understood or accepted by those around them.

To illustrate condigender identity, consider the story of Alex, who experiences their gender identity as a delicate whisper that is only heard in the quiet moments of solitude. In the solitude of nature, surrounded by the rustle of leaves and the gentle hum of the wind, Alex feels a profound sense of alignment with their true gender self. Yet, as soon as they reenter the cacophony of everyday life, their gender retreats into the shadows once more, leaving them to navigate the complexities of identity in a world that often demands clarity and certainty.

Through their journey, Alex learns to embrace the ephemeral nature of their gender identity with grace and acceptance, finding strength in the knowledge that their gender expression is as unique and nuanced as the circumstances that awaken it. Though they may face challenges along the way, Alex remains steadfast in their truth, knowing that their gender identity is valid and deserving of recognition and respect, no matter how fleeting or elusive it may seem.

Deliciagender individuals traverse the intricate landscape of gender identity with a flavor all their own, experiencing the sensation of embodying multiple genders while harboring a preference for one above the others. Imagine a delectable assortment of candies, each with its own unique flavor profile, yet one stands out as the favorite among the rest. Similarly, deliciagender individuals may feel a sense of resonance or affinity with multiple gender identities, yet find themselves drawn more strongly to one particular gender expression, which serves as the sweet spot of their identity.

Common experiences among deliciagender individuals include a sense of fluidity and versatility within their gender identity, as well as a preference or affinity for one specific gender over others. This preference may manifest in various ways, such as feeling more comfortable or authentic when expressing oneself within the context of the preferred gender, or experiencing a deeper sense of connection and resonance with the associated gender roles or characteristics.

Challenges faced by deliciagender individuals often revolve around navigating the complexities of their multifaceted gender identity within a society that often demands conformity to binary or monolithic gender norms. The nuanced nature of deliciagender identity may lead to feelings of confusion or uncertainty, as individuals grapple with reconciling their preference for one gender with the presence of multiple gender identities within themselves. Additionally, deliciagender individuals may encounter skepticism or misunderstanding from others who struggle to comprehend the subtleties of their identity.

To illustrate deliciagender identity, consider the story of Taylor, who experiences their gender identity as a sumptuous feast of flavors, each one tantalizing in its own right. While Taylor may feel a sense of alignment and authenticity across multiple gender identities, there is one particular gender expression that captivates their palate and leaves them craving more. Whether it's the comforting familiarity of masculinity, the vibrant energy of femininity, or the serene neutrality of nonbinary identity, Taylor finds solace and satisfaction in the sweet spot of their deliciagender identity.

Through their journey, Taylor learns to embrace the richness and complexity of their gender identity with gusto, finding strength in their ability to navigate the diverse flavors of self-expression with confidence and authenticity. Though they may encounter challenges along the way, Taylor remains steadfast in their truth, knowing that their deliciagender identity is valid and deserving of recognition and acceptance, no matter which flavor of gender they choose to savor.

Demifluid individuals navigate the intricate dance of gender identity with a unique blend of fluidity and stability, experiencing multiple genders where some are fluid while others remain static. Imagine a mosaic where some pieces shift and change with the flow of water, while others remain steadfast and immovable, creating a dynamic yet anchored sense of self. For demifluid individuals, certain aspects of their gender identity may fluctuate or evolve over time, while others remain constant and unwavering, providing a sense of grounding amidst the shifting currents of identity.

Common experiences among demifluid individuals include a deep awareness of the nuanced interplay between fluid and static elements within their gender identity. This may manifest as a sense of stability and consistency in certain aspects of their gender expression, while simultaneously experiencing moments of flux and transformation in others. For some, this dynamic blend of fluidity and stability offers a rich tapestry of self-expression, allowing for a holistic and authentic exploration of their gender identity.

Challenges faced by demifluid individuals often revolve around navigating the complexities of identity within a society that often seeks clear-cut labels and categories. The nuanced nature of demifluid identity may lead to feelings of confusion or uncertainty, as individuals grapple with reconciling the fluid and static elements of their gender expression. Additionally, demifluid individuals may encounter skepticism or misunderstanding from others who struggle to comprehend the intricacies of their identity, leading to feelings of invalidation or invisibility.

To illustrate demifluid identity, consider the story of Alex, who experiences their gender identity as a delicate balance between ebb and flow, stability and change. While certain aspects of Alex's gender remain constant and unchanging, providing a sense of grounding and continuity, others shift and evolve with the passage of time, reflecting the dynamic nature of their inner experience. Through self-reflection and self-awareness, Alex learns to embrace the complexities of their demifluid identity with grace and acceptance, finding strength in their ability to navigate the ever-shifting landscape of gender expression with confidence and authenticity.

Through their journey, Alex serves as a reminder of the beauty and richness of gender diversity, inviting others to explore and embrace the multifaceted nature of identity along the spectrum of gender. Though they may encounter challenges along the way, Alex remains steadfast in their truth, knowing that their demifluid identity is valid and deserving of recognition and acceptance, no matter how fluid or static it may seem.

Demiflux individuals navigate the complexities of gender identity with a unique blend of stability and fluidity, experiencing a combination of multiple genders where some remain static while others fluctuate in intensity. Picture a symphony where certain notes resonate with unwavering clarity, while others swell and diminish in a dynamic dance of expression. For demiflux individuals, certain aspects of their gender identity may remain constant and unchanging, providing a sense of grounding, while others ebb and flow in response to internal or external factors, reflecting the dynamic nature of their inner experience.

Demigender individuals, on the other hand, inhabit a space where gender is a mosaic of partial traits, blending elements of one gender with those of another. Imagine a painting where colors bleed into one another, creating a seamless tapestry of identity where boundaries blur and definitions dissolve. For demigender individuals, gender is not confined to rigid categories but rather exists on a spectrum where traits and characteristics from multiple genders coalesce to form a unique and authentic sense of self.

Common experiences among demiflux and demigender individuals include a deep sense of complexity and nuance within their gender identity. This may manifest as a continual process of self-exploration and self-discovery, as individuals navigate the interplay between static and fluctuating elements of their gender expression, as well as the blending of traits from multiple genders.

Challenges faced by demiflux and demigender individuals often revolve around navigating societal expectations and norms that may not fully encompass or validate the intricacies of their identity. This may lead to feelings of invisibility or invalidation, as well as difficulty finding spaces and communities where their identity is understood and accepted.

To illustrate demiflux and demigender identity, consider the story of Sam, who experiences a complex and multifaceted gender identity that defies simple categorization. Within Sam's experience, certain aspects of their gender remain consistent and unwavering, providing a sense of stability amidst the fluctuations of life. Yet, other aspects of their gender expression ebb and flow in response to internal or external factors, reflecting the dynamic nature of their inner experience. Additionally, Sam's gender is characterized by a blending of traits from multiple genders, creating a rich tapestry of identity that defies traditional binaries and labels.

Through their journey, Sam learns to embrace the complexities and nuances of their demiflux and demigender identity with grace and authenticity, finding strength in their ability to navigate the intricacies of gender expression with confidence and resilience. Though they may encounter challenges along the way, Sam remains steadfast in their truth, knowing that their identity is valid and deserving of recognition and acceptance, no matter how complex or fluid it may seem.

Domgender individuals navigate the intricate landscape of gender identity with one gender dominating over the others, creating a sense of hierarchy or prominence within their sense of self. Picture a majestic tree towering over a forest, its branches reaching skyward while other trees stand in its shadow. Similarly, for domgender individuals, one gender asserts itself as the primary or dominant aspect of their identity, overshadowing the presence of other genders that may coexist within them. This dominant gender may exert a strong influence over the individual's thoughts, feelings, and expressions, shaping their sense of self in profound ways.

Common experiences among domgender individuals include a deep sense of alignment and authenticity with the dominant gender, as well as a recognition of the presence of other genders within their identity. This may manifest as a feeling of resonance or affinity with the dominant gender, while simultaneously acknowledging the complexity and diversity of their gender expression. Challenges faced by domgender individuals often revolve around navigating the interplay between the dominant gender and other genders within their identity. This may lead to feelings of internal conflict or confusion, as individuals grapple with reconciling the prominence of one gender with the presence of others that may not align as strongly with their sense of self.

To illustrate domgender identity, consider the story of Alex, who experiences their gender identity as a towering presence that casts a long shadow over the landscape of their self-expression.

For Alex, one gender asserts itself as the dominant aspect of their identity, exerting a powerful influence over their thoughts, feelings, and behaviors. Despite the presence of other genders within their identity, it is the dominant gender that holds sway, shaping their sense of self in profound and undeniable ways. Through self-reflection and self-awareness, Alex learns to embrace the complexities of their domgender identity with grace and acceptance, finding strength in their ability to navigate the hierarchy of their gender expression with confidence and authenticity. Though they may encounter challenges along the way, Alex remains steadfast in their truth, knowing that their dominant gender is valid and deserving of recognition and acceptance, no matter the presence of other genders within their identity.

Duragender individuals navigate the intricacies of gender identity with the presence of more than one gender, where one endures for a longer duration than the others. This enduring gender serves as a cornerstone of their identity, providing a sense of continuity and stability amidst the flux of gender expression. Imagine a sturdy bridge spanning a river, with one pillar firmly rooted in the earth while others rise and fall with the currents. Similarly, for duragender individuals, one gender remains steadfast and enduring, anchoring their sense of self even as other genders may come and go over time.

Common experiences among duragender individuals include a deep sense of connection and resonance with the enduring gender, as well as an awareness of the transient nature of other genders within their identity. This may manifest as a feeling of stability and authenticity when expressing oneself within the context of the enduring gender, while simultaneously navigating the ebb and flow of other genders that may arise and dissipate over time.

Challenges faced by duragender individuals often revolve around navigating the dynamic nature of their gender identity within a society that may not fully understand or recognize the complexities of their experience. This may lead to feelings of confusion or uncertainty, as individuals grapple with reconciling the enduring nature of one gender with the presence of others that may not endure as long or as strongly.

Duragender individuals may also face challenges related to self-validation and acceptance, as they seek to honor and embrace the full spectrum of their gender identity, including both the enduring and transient aspects. Additionally, duragender individuals may encounter skepticism or misunderstanding from others who struggle to comprehend the intricacies of their identity, leading to feelings of invalidation or invisibility.

Despite these challenges, duragender individuals find strength and resilience in their ability to navigate the complexities of their gender identity with grace and authenticity. Through self-reflection and self-acceptance, they learn to embrace the fullness of their identity, honoring both the enduring and transient aspects of their gender expression. Though they may encounter obstacles along the way, duragender individuals remain steadfast in their truth, knowing that their identity is valid and deserving of recognition and acceptance, no matter the duration or intensity of their genders.

Egogender is a deeply personal and introspective form of gender identity, uniquely identified and understood by the individual alone. Unlike traditional gender categories that may be influenced by societal norms or external factors, egogender is rooted solely in the individual's subjective experience within themselves. Imagine a private garden hidden away from the world, where the flowers bloom and the trees sway to the rhythm of the individual's innermost thoughts and feelings. Similarly, for egogender individuals, their gender identity is cultivated and nurtured within the sanctuary of their own mind and soul, unaffected by external influences or expectations.

Common experiences among egogender individuals include a profound sense of ownership and autonomy over their gender identity, as well as a deep connection to the unique nuances and complexities of their inner experience. This may manifest as a feeling of empowerment and authenticity when expressing oneself within the context of their egogender, free from the constraints of societal norms or expectations. Challenges faced by egogender individuals often revolve around navigating the disconnect between their internal sense of gender and external perceptions or categorizations. This may lead to feelings of isolation or invalidation, as individuals struggle to articulate or validate their gender identity in a world that may not fully understand or recognize the complexities of their experience.

To illustrate egogender identity, consider the story of Jamie, who experiences their gender identity as a deeply personal and intimate aspect of their being. For Jamie, their egogender is a sacred space where they can explore and embrace the fullness of their identity, free from the judgments or expectations of others. Through self-reflection and self-discovery, Jamie learns to honor and celebrate the unique nuances and complexities of their egogender, finding strength and resilience in their ability to navigate the intricacies of gender identity with grace and authenticity. Though they may encounter challenges along the way, Jamie remains steadfast in their truth, knowing that their egogender is valid and deserving of recognition and acceptance, no matter the perceptions or expectations of the world around them.

Epicene individuals navigate the realm of gender with a profound sense of detachment from the binary constructs of male and female, feeling unable to fully relate to either set of characteristics. Picture a traveler wandering through a vast and diverse landscape, observing the myriad facets of gender expression with a sense of curiosity and detachment. Similarly, for epicene individuals, their gender identity exists beyond the confines of traditional binaries, encompassing a spectrum of traits and expressions that defy easy categorization.

Common experiences among epicene individuals include a deep sense of ambiguity and fluidity within their gender identity, as well as a feeling of disconnection from societal expectations or norms related to gender. This may manifest as a sense of liberation and empowerment, as individuals embrace the freedom to define and express their gender on their own terms, free from the constraints of binary thinking. Challenges faced by epicene individuals often revolve around navigating a world that may not fully understand or accept the complexity of their gender identity. This may lead to feelings of isolation or alienation, as individuals struggle to find validation and acceptance for their authentic selves amidst a society that often seeks to impose rigid gender roles and categories.

To illustrate epicene identity, consider the story of Jackson, who experiences their gender as a vast and boundless expanse, free from the confines of binary constraints. For Jackson, gender is not a fixed point on a spectrum but rather a fluid and ever-evolving journey of self-discovery and expression. Through introspection and self-reflection, Jackson learns to embrace the ambiguity and fluidity of their epicene identity with courage and authenticity, finding strength in their ability to navigate the complexities of gender identity with grace and resilience. Though they may encounter challenges along the way, Jackson remains steadfast in their truth, knowing that their epicene identity is valid and deserving of recognition and acceptance, no matter the expectations or perceptions of others.

Esspigender individuals forge a unique connection between their gender identity and the realm of spirits, drawing inspiration and understanding from the spiritual world. Imagine a tapestry woven with threads of ethereal energy, each strand representing the presence of spiritual beings that shape and inform the individual's sense of self. For esspigender individuals, gender is not solely a product of human experience but is intertwined with the wisdom and energy of the spiritual realm, imbuing their identity with a sense of depth and transcendence.

Common experiences among esspigender individuals include a profound sense of resonance and alignment with the energies and characteristics of specific spirits or spiritual entities. This may manifest as a feeling of kinship or connection with the spiritual beings that inform their gender identity, as well as a deep sense of reverence and respect for the wisdom and guidance they provide. Challenges faced by esspigender individuals often revolve around navigating a world that may not fully understand or accept the complexity of their spiritual identity. This may lead to feelings of isolation or alienation, as individuals struggle to find validation and acceptance for their authentic selves amidst a society that may dismiss or misunderstand their spiritual beliefs.

To illustrate esspigender identity, consider the story of Jamie, who experiences their gender identity as intimately intertwined with the presence of spiritual beings. For Jamie, gender is not just a product of human experience but is deeply influenced by the energies and wisdom of the spirits that guide and inspire them. Through meditation and introspection, Jamie learns to embrace the spiritual aspects of their gender identity with reverence and gratitude, finding strength and solace in the knowledge that they are connected to something greater than themselves. Though they may encounter challenges along the way, Jamie remains steadfast in their truth, knowing that their esspigender identity is valid and deserving of recognition and acceptance, no matter the perceptions or expectations of others.

Exgender individuals navigate the landscape of gender identity with a profound sense of detachment and disassociation from any gender on the spectrum. Picture a blank canvas untouched by the strokes of gendered expectations, where the absence of identity becomes a form of liberation and empowerment. For exgender individuals, the denial to identify with any gender serves as a declaration of autonomy and self-determination, freeing them from the constraints of societal norms and expectations.

Common experiences among exgender individuals include a deep sense of relief and authenticity in embracing their genderlessness, as well as a feeling of liberation from the pressures to conform to binary or non-binary gender categories. This may manifest as a sense of freedom and empowerment, as individuals reclaim agency over their own identity and assert their right to exist beyond the confines of gendered labels. Challenges faced by exgender individuals often revolve around navigating a world that may not fully understand or accept the concept of genderlessness. This may lead to feelings of isolation or invalidation, as individuals struggle to find validation and acceptance for their authentic selves amidst a society that often seeks to impose rigid gender roles and expectations.

To illustrate exgender identity, consider the story of Jessica, who experiences their gender identity as a blank slate, free from the constraints of gendered expectations or categories. For Jessica, the denial to identify with any gender serves as a form of empowerment and liberation, allowing them to embrace the fullness of their identity without the limitations of societal labels. Through self-reflection and self-acceptance, Jessica learns to celebrate the uniqueness of their genderlessness, finding strength and resilience in their ability to navigate the complexities of identity with grace and authenticity. Though they may encounter challenges along the way, Jessica remains steadfast in their truth, knowing that their exgender identity is valid and deserving of recognition and acceptance, no matter the perceptions or expectations of others.

Existigender individuals experience their gender identity as something that only comes into existence when they actively make conscious efforts to realize it. Imagine a flickering flame that illuminates the darkness only when sparked to life; similarly, for existigender individuals, their gender identity emerges from the shadows of consciousness when they intentionally focus their attention on it. This identity is not a constant presence but rather a transient phenomenon that manifests in moments of self-reflection and introspection.

Common experiences among existigender individuals include a sense of fluidity and variability in their gender identity, as well as a feeling of agency and control over its manifestation. This may manifest as a deep sense of empowerment, as individuals navigate the process of self-discovery and identity formation with intentionality and mindfulness. Challenges faced by existigender individuals often revolve around navigating the fluctuating nature of their gender identity within a world that may not fully understand or accept the concept of gender as a fluid and dynamic construct. This may lead to feelings of confusion or invalidation, as individuals struggle to articulate or validate their identity in a society that often seeks to impose rigid categories and labels.

To illustrate existigender identity, consider the story of Sam, who experiences their gender identity as something that comes into existence only when they actively engage in self-reflection and introspection. For Sam, gender is not a fixed or static concept but rather a fluid and dynamic phenomenon that ebbs and flows with their conscious awareness. Through intentional reflection and mindfulness, Sam learns to embrace the fluidity and variability of their existigender identity, finding strength and resilience in their ability to navigate the complexities of identity with grace and authenticity. Though they may encounter challenges along the way, Sam remains steadfast in their truth, knowing that their existigender identity is valid and deserving of recognition and acceptance, no matter the perceptions or expectations of others.

Femfluid individuals experience a fluid or fluctuating relationship with feminine genders, where their sense of femininity ebbs and flows over time. Picture a river whose currents shift and change with the tides, reflecting the dynamic nature of femininity within the individual's identity. For femfluid individuals, their connection to femininity is not fixed or static but rather evolves and transforms in response to internal and external influences.

Common experiences among femfluid individuals include a sense of flexibility and adaptability in their gender expression, as well as a feeling of empowerment in embracing the fluidity of their femininity. This may manifest as a deep sense of liberation, as individuals navigate the process of self-discovery and self-expression with authenticity and confidence. Challenges faced by femfluid individuals often revolve around navigating a world that may not fully understand or accept the concept of gender fluidity. This may lead to feelings of invalidation or invisibility, as individuals struggle to find validation and acceptance for their authentic selves amidst a society that often seeks to impose rigid gender norms and expectations.

To illustrate femfluid identity, consider the story of Mark, who experiences their relationship with femininity as fluid and dynamic, shifting and evolving over time. For Mark, femininity is not a fixed or immutable characteristic but rather a multifaceted aspect of their identity that adapts and changes in response to their innermost feelings and experiences.

Femgender is a nonbinary gender identity characterized by a strong association with femininity. Individuals who identify as femgender may experience a deep sense of alignment with feminine traits, expressions, and roles, while simultaneously rejecting the notion of strictly adhering to a binary understanding of gender.

Common experiences among femgender individuals include a feeling of resonance and authenticity when expressing themselves in ways traditionally associated with femininity, such as through clothing, mannerisms, or interests. They may also experience a sense of liberation in embracing their nonbinary identity while still connecting with aspects of femininity. However, challenges may arise when navigating societal expectations and misconceptions surrounding gender. Femgender individuals may face discrimination or invalidation from those who fail to understand or accept the nuanced nature of their identity. Additionally, they may struggle to find representation and inclusion within communities that predominantly focus on binary gender narratives.

Despite these challenges, femgender individuals often find strength and empowerment in embracing their unique identity, forging connections with others who share similar experiences, and advocating for greater understanding and acceptance of nonbinary genders within society. Through self-discovery and self-acceptance, they navigate the complexities of gender identity with resilience and authenticity, knowing that their femgender identity is valid and deserving of recognition.

Fluidflux is a gender identity characterized by fluidity between two or more genders, accompanied by fluctuations in the intensity of those genders over time. Individuals who identify as fluidflux may experience shifts in their gender expression and identity, moving between different genders with varying degrees of intensity.

Common experiences among fluidflux individuals include a dynamic sense of self, where their gender identity evolves and changes in response to internal and external factors. They may feel comfortable and aligned with multiple genders at different times, experiencing a sense of fluidity in their gender expression. Additionally, fluidflux individuals may notice fluctuations in the intensity of their gender identities, with some genders feeling more prominent or pronounced than others at certain points in time.

Challenges faced by fluidflux individuals often revolve around navigating the complexity and fluidity of their gender identity within a society that may not fully understand or accept nonbinary experiences. They may encounter difficulty in finding language to describe their identity, as well as skepticism or invalidation from those who adhere to binary notions of gender. Additionally, fluidflux individuals may struggle with feelings of uncertainty or instability in their sense of self, as their gender identity evolves and changes over time.

Despite these challenges, fluidflux individuals often find strength and empowerment in embracing the fluidity of their gender identity, forging connections with others who share similar experiences, and advocating for greater visibility and acceptance of nonbinary genders within society. Through self-exploration and self-acceptance, they navigate the complexities of gender identity with resilience and authenticity, knowing that their fluidflux identity is valid and deserving of recognition.

Gemigender is a unique gender identity characterized by the coexistence of two genders that are opposite in nature, yet they flux and work together harmoniously within the individual's sense of self. Unlike binary identities, gemigender individuals experience a dynamic interplay between these contrasting genders, with each informing and complementing the other in a fluid and cohesive manner.

Common experiences among gemigender individuals include a deep sense of balance and integration between their two opposing genders, as well as a feeling of wholeness and completeness in embracing the complexity of their identity. They may navigate their gender expression with a sense of fluidity, seamlessly shifting between different aspects of their gender identity depending on the context or their own internal fluctuations.

Challenges faced by gemigender individuals often revolve around navigating societal expectations and misconceptions surrounding gender. They may encounter difficulty in finding language to describe their unique identity, as well as skepticism or invalidation from those who struggle to understand the nuanced nature of their experience. Additionally, gemigender individuals may grapple with feelings of internal conflict or confusion as they strive to reconcile the opposing aspects of their gender identity.

Despite these challenges, gemigender individuals often find strength and empowerment in embracing the complexity of their identity, forging connections with others who share similar experiences, and advocating for greater visibility and acceptance of nonbinary genders within society. Through self-exploration and self-acceptance, they navigate the intricacies of gender identity with resilience and authenticity, knowing that their gemigender identity is valid and deserving of recognition.

Genderblank is a gender identity closely related to a blank space, representing a feeling of emptiness or absence of gender. Individuals who identify as genderblank may experience a sense of detachment or neutrality towards traditional gender categories, perceiving their gender identity as undefined or indeterminate.

Common experiences among genderblank individuals include a feeling of disconnection from societal expectations and norms surrounding gender, as well as a sense of freedom from the constraints of binary thinking. They may navigate their gender identity with a sense of neutrality or ambivalence, feeling neither strongly aligned with masculinity nor femininity.

Challenges faced by genderblank individuals often revolve around navigating a world that may not fully understand or accept the concept of a gender identity that exists outside of traditional categories. They may encounter difficulty in finding language to describe their identity, as well as skepticism or invalidation from those who struggle to understand the nuanced nature of their experience. Additionally, genderblank individuals may grapple with feelings of isolation or invisibility within communities that predominantly focus on binary gender narratives.

Genderflow and **genderfluidity** are both nonbinary gender identities that encompass fluidity and variability in gender experience. However, there are subtle distinctions between the two.

Genderflow individuals experience their gender identity as fluid and dynamic, flowing between infinite feelings and expressions without adherence to fixed categories or labels. Their gender may change and evolve continuously, encompassing a wide range of experiences and emotions that transcend traditional notions of gender.

On the other hand, genderfluid individuals also experience fluidity in their gender identity but may not necessarily flow between infinite feelings. Instead, they may fluctuate between multiple distinct genders, experiencing each one with varying degrees of intensity over time. These genders may be fixed or stable identities within the individual's gender spectrum, rather than an endless array of possibilities.

Common experiences among both genderflow and genderfluid individuals include a sense of fluidity and variability in their gender expression, as well as a feeling of liberation in embracing the complexity of their identity. They may navigate their gender identity with a sense of flexibility and adaptability, embracing the freedom to express themselves authentically across a diverse range of genders.

Challenges faced by genderflow and genderfluid individuals often revolve around navigating societal expectations and norms surrounding gender. They may encounter difficulty in finding validation and acceptance for their fluid identities, as well as skepticism or invalidation from those who struggle to understand the nuanced nature of their experience. Additionally, they may grapple with feelings of uncertainty or instability in their sense of self, as their gender identity evolves and changes over time.

Genderfuzz is a nonbinary gender identity characterized by the blending or blurring together of multiple genders, resulting in a sense of ambiguity or indistinctness in one's gender identity. Individuals who identify as genderfuzz may experience their gender as a fuzzy or nebulous concept, with various gender identities merging and overlapping in complex and fluid ways.

Common experiences among genderfuzz individuals include a feeling of ambiguity or uncertainty regarding their gender identity, as well as a sense of fluidity and variability in their gender expression. They may navigate their gender identity with a sense of flexibility and adaptability, embracing the complexity of their identity without adhering to rigid categories or labels.

Challenges faced by genderfuzz individuals often revolve around navigating societal expectations and norms surrounding gender. They may encounter difficulty in finding language to describe their identity, as well as skepticism or invalidation from those who struggle to understand the nuanced nature of their experience. Additionally, genderfuzz individuals may grapple with feelings of confusion or frustration as they strive to reconcile the blending of multiple genders within their identity.

Genderflux is a nonbinary gender identity characterized by fluctuations in the intensity of one's gender over time. Individuals who identify as genderflux may experience shifts in the strength or intensity of their gender identity, with feelings of gender ranging from strong and prominent to weak or nonexistent.

Common characteristics of genderflux include a dynamic and ever-changing relationship with one's gender identity, as well as a sense of variability and fluidity in gender expression. Genderflux individuals may navigate their gender identity with a sense of flexibility and adaptability, embracing the fluctuations in their gender experience without adhering to fixed categories or labels.

Experiences commonly shared among genderflux individuals include periods of feeling deeply connected to and aligned with their gender, as well as moments of feeling disconnected or distant from their gender identity. These fluctuations in gender intensity may occur gradually over time or suddenly and unpredictably, leading to a sense of uncertainty or instability in one's sense of self.

Challenges faced by genderflux individuals often revolve around navigating the variability and unpredictability of their gender experience within a society that may not fully understand or accept nonbinary identities. They may encounter difficulty in finding language to describe their identity, as well as skepticism or invalidation from those who struggle to understand the nuanced nature of their experience.

Genderpuck is a nonbinary gender identity characterized by a deliberate resistance to conform to societal norms and expectations surrounding gender. Individuals who identify as genderpuck may reject traditional gender roles, expressions, and labels, opting instead to define their gender identity on their own terms.

Common characteristics of genderpuck include a sense of defiance and rebellion against binary notions of gender, as well as a desire to challenge and subvert societal expectations surrounding gender. Genderpuck individuals may navigate their gender identity with a sense of freedom and autonomy, embracing the opportunity to carve out their own unique identity separate from the constraints of traditional gender norms.

Experiences commonly shared among genderpuck individuals include a feeling of empowerment in embracing their nonconformity, as well as a sense of solidarity with other marginalized genders and identities. They may actively resist gendered expectations and stereotypes, advocating for greater acceptance and visibility of nonbinary genders within society.

Challenges faced by genderpuck individuals often revolve around navigating societal pushback and discrimination for their refusal to adhere to traditional gender norms. They may encounter resistance or invalidation from those who struggle to understand or accept the validity of nonbinary identities, as well as face discrimination or marginalization in various social contexts.

Genderqueer is a nonbinary gender identity characterized by a deliberate blurring or challenging of preconceived boundaries surrounding gender, particularly in relation to the gender binary or the concept of having just one gender type. Individuals who identify as genderqueer may reject or transcend traditional notions of gender, embracing a fluid and multifaceted understanding of their own identity.

Common characteristics of genderqueer include a sense of ambiguity or fluidity in one's gender identity, as well as a rejection of rigid gender categories and labels. Genderqueer individuals may navigate their gender identity with a sense of freedom and autonomy, embracing the opportunity to define themselves outside of societal expectations.

Experiences commonly shared among genderqueer individuals include a feeling of empowerment in embracing their nonconformity, as well as a sense of solidarity with other marginalized genders and identities. They may actively challenge gendered expectations and stereotypes, advocating for greater recognition and acceptance of nonbinary genders within society.

Challenges faced by genderqueer individuals often revolve around navigating societal pushback and discrimination for their refusal to adhere to traditional gender norms. They may encounter resistance or invalidation from those who struggle to understand or accept the validity of nonbinary identities, as well as face discrimination or marginalization in various social contexts.

Gender witched is a nonbinary gender identity characterized by a sense of inclination toward the notion of having one gender, yet uncertainty or ambiguity regarding which gender that may be. Individuals who identify as gender witched may experience a complex and multifaceted relationship with gender, grappling with feelings of indecision or fluidity in their sense of self.

Common characteristics of gender witched include a feeling of being drawn toward the concept of having one gender, yet experiencing difficulty in identifying or defining that gender definitively. Gender witched individuals may navigate their gender identity with a sense of exploration and introspection, embracing the opportunity to explore and understand their own identity on their own terms.

Experiences commonly shared among gender witched individuals include a feeling of uncertainty or confusion regarding their gender identity, as well as a sense of curiosity and discovery in exploring different aspects of themselves. They may actively engage in self-reflection and self-exploration, seeking to better understand and define their own unique identity separate from societal expectations.

Challenges faced by gender witched individuals often revolve around navigating feelings of ambiguity or uncertainty in a world that may prioritize binary understandings of gender. They may encounter difficulty in finding language to describe their identity, as well as skepticism or invalidation from those who struggle to understand the nuanced nature of their experience.

Girlflux is a gender identity where the individual primarily identifies as female, but experiences fluctuating intensities of female identity over time. This variance can range from feeling strongly connected to their femininity to experiencing moments of neutrality or even detachment from it.

Common characteristics of girlflux include a dynamic and evolving relationship with femininity, where the individual's sense of female identity shifts in intensity or prominence. Girlflux individuals may navigate their gender identity with a sense of flexibility and adaptability, embracing the fluidity of their experience without adhering strictly to binary or fixed categories.

Experiences commonly shared among girlflux individuals include a feeling of empowerment in embracing the complexity of their identity, as well as a sense of liberation in acknowledging the variability of their gender expression. They may actively explore and celebrate different facets of femininity, embracing the diversity of their experience while also recognizing the validity of their fluctuating gender identity.

Challenges faced by girlflux individuals often revolve around navigating societal expectations and norms surrounding gender. They may encounter difficulty in finding validation and acceptance for their fluid identity, as well as skepticism or invalidation from those who struggle to understand the nuanced nature of their experience. Additionally, girlflux individuals may grapple with feelings of uncertainty or confusion as they strive to reconcile the variability of their gender identity with societal expectations of consistency and stability.

Healgender is a gender identity characterized by a profound sense of peace, calm, and positivity. Individuals who identify as healgender experience their gender as a source of comfort and healing, bringing them solace and inner tranquility.

Common characteristics of healgender include a deep connection to one's gender identity as a source of strength and empowerment. Healgender individuals may find that their gender brings them a sense of emotional well-being and resilience, serving as a source of positivity and hope in their lives.

Experiences commonly shared among healgender individuals include a feeling of alignment with their true self and a sense of harmony with their gender identity. They may navigate their gender with a sense of gratitude and appreciation, recognizing the healing power that their identity brings to their life.

Challenges faced by healgender individuals may include navigating societal expectations and norms surrounding gender, as well as dealing with potential misunderstandings or misconceptions about their identity. However, healgender individuals often find strength and resilience in embracing the positivity and healing energy of their gender identity, forging connections with others who share similar experiences and advocating for greater understanding and acceptance of diverse gender identities within society.

Mirrorgender is a gender identity characterized by the tendency to change one's gender expression or identity based on the individuals or groups one is surrounded by. Individuals who identify as mirrorgender may find that their sense of gender fluctuates in response to the people they interact with, reflecting the social context and dynamics of their environment.

Common characteristics of mirrorgender include a fluid and adaptive relationship with gender, where one's gender identity may shift to align with the perceived expectations or norms of those around them. Mirrorgender individuals may navigate their gender identity with a sense of flexibility and adaptability, adjusting their expression or identity to fit the social context in which they find themselves.

Experiences commonly shared among mirrorgender individuals include a feeling of fluidity and variability in their gender expression, as well as a sense of responsiveness to the social cues and dynamics of their environment. They may find that their gender identity is influenced by the people they interact with, leading to shifts in their sense of self and expression.

Challenges faced by mirrorgender individuals often revolve around navigating the complexity of their identity within different social contexts. They may encounter difficulty in maintaining a consistent sense of self across various situations, as well as feelings of confusion or uncertainty about their authentic identity amidst the influence of external factors.

Omnigender is a gender identity characterized by the experience of encompassing or connecting with all genders. Individuals who identify as omnigender may perceive themselves as existing beyond or transcending traditional binary understandings of gender, embracing the full spectrum of gender diversity.

Common characteristics of omnigender include a profound sense of inclusivity and expansiveness in one's gender identity, where all genders are seen as valid and interconnected. Omnigender individuals may navigate their gender identity with a sense of openness and acceptance, recognizing and honoring the diversity of gender expressions and experiences.

Experiences commonly shared among omnigender individuals include a feeling of connection to multiple gender identities, as well as a sense of fluidity and flexibility in their own sense of self. They may find that their gender identity is dynamic and evolving, encompassing a wide range of feelings and expressions that transcend traditional categories or labels.

Challenges faced by omnigender individuals often revolve around navigating societal expectations and norms surrounding gender. They may encounter resistance or invalidation from those who struggle to understand or accept the validity of nonbinary identities, as well as face discrimination or marginalization in various social contexts.

Disability further intersects with gender, shaping the lived experiences of individuals with disabilities across the gender spectrum. Disabled gender-diverse individuals may face additional barriers to accessing affirming healthcare, navigating social spaces, and participating fully in society. Moreover, ableism within LGBTQ+ communities can exacerbate feelings of exclusion and marginalization for disabled gender-diverse individuals, further complicating their sense of identity and belonging.

Socioeconomic status also plays a significant role in shaping how individuals experience gender. Transgender individuals, especially those from marginalized communities, often face economic hardship due to discrimination in employment and housing, as well as limited access to healthcare and social services. This economic vulnerability intersects with gender to compound the challenges faced by transgender individuals, creating barriers to safety, security, and well-being.

Intersectionality invites us to consider the ways in which systems of power and privilege intersect to shape individual experiences and identities. It challenges us to move beyond simplistic understandings of gender and recognize the multiple, intersecting factors that influence how gender is experienced and understood. By centering the experiences of marginalized individuals and amplifying their voices, we can work towards creating more inclusive and equitable spaces for all gender-diverse people.

Navigating intersecting identities is a multifaceted journey that shapes the lived experiences of individuals in profound ways. Whether it's the convergence of gender and race, sexuality and disability, or any combination thereof, the unique experiences of individuals with intersecting identities are influenced by the complex interplay of social, cultural, and structural factors.

For individuals who occupy multiple marginalized identities, such as being a transgender person of color or a disabled queer individual, their experiences are often shaped by the compounded effects of discrimination and marginalization. Black transgender women, for example, face intersecting forms of violence and discrimination due to their gender identity and racial identity. They are disproportionately affected by hate crimes, police brutality, and systemic barriers to accessing healthcare, housing, and employment. This intersectionality of race and gender magnifies the challenges faced by Black transgender women, highlighting the urgent need for comprehensive and intersectional approaches to addressing systemic inequities.

Similarly, the experiences of disabled LGBTQ+ individuals are shaped by the intersection of disability and sexuality. Disabled queer individuals may face unique barriers to accessing affirming healthcare, navigating social spaces, and forming intimate relationships. They may also encounter ableism within LGBTQ+ communities, which can manifest in the form of exclusion, tokenization, or the erasure of disabled experiences.

This intersectionality underscores the importance of recognizing and addressing the diverse needs and experiences of disabled LGBTQ+ individuals within both disability and LGBTQ+ advocacy spaces.

Moreover, the intersecting identities of individuals with marginalized sexual orientations, gender identities, and socioeconomic statuses compound their experiences of discrimination and marginalization. LGBTQ+ individuals who also face economic hardship may encounter additional barriers to accessing affirming healthcare, securing stable housing, and pursuing education and employment opportunities. This intersectionality of sexuality, gender, and socioeconomic status highlights the intersecting forms of oppression faced by individuals at the margins of society and underscores the need for inclusive and intersectional approaches to addressing systemic inequalities.

In addition to facing multiple forms of discrimination and marginalization, individuals with intersecting identities also navigate complex internal struggles related to identity, belonging, and self-acceptance. They may grapple with feelings of invisibility, isolation, or internalized stigma as they navigate the intersecting layers of their identity. Moreover, they may struggle to find affirming spaces and communities where they can fully express themselves without fear of judgment or rejection.

Despite the challenges they face, individuals with intersecting identities also possess unique strengths and resilience that emerge from their diverse experiences and perspectives.

They often bring a wealth of insight, creativity, and resilience to their communities and movements for social change. By centering the voices and experiences of individuals with intersecting identities, we can work towards creating more inclusive and equitable spaces that honor the complexity and diversity of human identity.

Examining privilege and oppression within gender dynamics unveils the intricate web of power dynamics that shape individuals' experiences based on their gender identity. In patriarchal societies, cisgender men often hold privilege due to their alignment with societal norms and expectations surrounding masculinity. This privilege manifests in various forms, including greater access to economic opportunities, political power, and social influence. For example, men are more likely to hold leadership positions in corporations and governments, with women and gender-diverse individuals facing systemic barriers to advancement. Additionally, cisgender men often enjoy greater freedom of movement and expression without fear of gender-based violence or discrimination, highlighting the intersecting dynamics of gender and safety.

Conversely, women and gender-diverse individuals often face systemic oppression and discrimination due to their gender identity. Women, in particular, experience gender-based disparities in areas such as pay, healthcare, and representation in leadership roles. The gender pay gap, for instance, persists across industries and occupations, with women earning less than their male counterparts for equal work.

Moreover, gender-based violence, including sexual harassment and domestic abuse, disproportionately affects women and gender-diverse individuals, perpetuating cycles of trauma and harm. Transgender and nonbinary individuals also face unique forms of discrimination and violence, including denial of healthcare, housing, and employment opportunities, further exacerbating their vulnerability to systemic oppression.

Intersectionality further complicates the dynamics of privilege and oppression within gender dynamics, as individuals with intersecting marginalized identities may face compounded forms of discrimination and marginalization. For example, transgender women of color experience intersecting forms of racism, sexism, and transphobia, resulting in disproportionately high rates of violence, poverty, and incarceration. Similarly, disabled women may face barriers to accessing healthcare, education, and employment due to the intersection of ableism and sexism. These examples underscore the importance of intersectional approaches to addressing systemic inequalities and dismantling systems of oppression that perpetuate gender-based discrimination and marginalization.

Moreover, privilege and oppression within gender dynamics are perpetuated and reinforced by societal norms, cultural attitudes, and institutional policies that uphold traditional gender roles and hierarchies. Gender socialization begins at an early age, with children being socialized into binary gender norms that dictate how they should behave, express themselves, and interact with others.

These norms not only constrain individuals' freedom and autonomy but also perpetuate harmful stereotypes and biases that contribute to gender-based discrimination and violence.

Understanding and respecting diverse gender identities is essential for creating inclusive and affirming environments where everyone can feel seen, valued, and respected. In everyday life, individuals encounter a wide range of gender expressions and identities, and it's important to approach these interactions with empathy, openness, and a willingness to learn. Here are some practical pieces of advice for navigating gender in everyday life:

1. Educate Yourself: Take the initiative to educate yourself about different gender identities and expressions. Read books, articles, and resources written by gender-diverse individuals, and seek out educational opportunities such as workshops or seminars on gender diversity.

2. Use Inclusive Language: Be mindful of the language you use when referring to individuals' gender identities. Use inclusive language that respects people's self-identified gender, pronouns, and names. Avoid making assumptions about someone's gender based on their appearance or presentation, and always ask for and use the pronouns that individuals prefer. If you're unsure of someone's pronouns, it's okay to politely ask for clarification.

3. Respect Boundaries: Respect individuals' boundaries when it comes to discussing their gender identity. Avoid prying or intrusive questions about someone's gender identity or transition process, and refrain from making insensitive or inappropriate comments.

Instead, focus on creating a supportive space where individuals feel comfortable expressing themselves authentically.

4. Listen and Learn: Take the time to listen to the experiences and perspectives of gender-diverse individuals without judgment or interruption. Create space for people to share their stories and insights and be willing to learn from their experiences. By listening and learning from gender-diverse voices, we can gain a deeper understanding of the complexities of gender identity and expression.

Navigating gender in everyday life requires a commitment to understanding, respect, and inclusion. By educating ourselves, using inclusive language, respecting boundaries, challenging gender norms, advocating for inclusive policies, listening and learning, and being allies to gender-diverse individuals, we can create more affirming and equitable environments where everyone can thrive. Together, we can build a world that honors and celebrates the rich diversity of human gender expression and identity.

Creating inclusive environments in various settings requires proactive efforts to ensure that all individuals, regardless of gender identity, feel valued, respected, and supported. Here are some tips for fostering inclusivity in workplaces, schools, healthcare settings, and beyond:

Workplaces:

1. Implement Inclusive Policies: Establish policies that explicitly prohibit discrimination based on gender identity and expression. This may include policies related to hiring, promotion, dress code, restroom access, and healthcare benefits. Ensure that these policies are clearly communicated to all employees and enforced consistently.

2. Provide Training: Offer training sessions for staff on topics related to gender diversity and inclusion. This may include education on terminology, pronoun usage, respectful communication, and strategies for creating inclusive work environments. Encourage ongoing dialogue and learning among employees to foster a culture of inclusivity.

3. Offer Gender-Neutral Facilities: Provide gender-neutral restroom facilities to accommodate individuals of all gender identities. Ensure that these facilities are accessible, safe, and well-maintained. Consider other aspects of the workplace environment, such as locker rooms and changing areas, to ensure inclusivity for all employees.

4. Respect Privacy and Confidentiality: Respect the privacy and confidentiality of employees' gender identity and expression. Avoid disclosing sensitive information without consent and ensure that all employees feel comfortable sharing their gender identity or seeking support if needed.

Healthcare Settings:

1. Offer Culturally Competent Care: Provide culturally competent and affirming care for patients of all gender identities. Train healthcare providers on best practices for addressing the unique healthcare needs of transgender, nonbinary, and gender-nonconforming individuals.

2. Use Inclusive Language: Use inclusive language when interacting with patients, including asking for and using their preferred name and pronouns. Avoid making assumptions about patients' gender identity or medical history and respect their autonomy in making decisions about their healthcare.

3. Provide Accessible Services: Ensure that healthcare facilities are accessible to individuals of all gender identities, including providing gender-neutral restroom facilities and accommodating the specific needs of transgender and gender-nonconforming patients. Offer resources and referrals for specialized care, such as hormone therapy or gender-affirming surgery.

4. Foster Trust and Respect: Foster a trusting and respectful environment where patients feel comfortable discussing their gender identity and healthcare needs openly. Listen to patients' concerns and experiences without expressing judgment and work collaboratively with them to develop personalized treatment plans that meet their needs and goals.

Overall, creating inclusive environments in workplaces, schools, healthcare settings, and beyond requires a commitment to understanding, respect, and advocacy for gender diversity and inclusion. By implementing inclusive policies, providing education and training, offering supportive resources and services, and fostering a culture of respect and acceptance, we can create environments where all individuals feel valued, respected, and empowered to be their authentic selves.

Throughout this book, we've embarked on a journey to explore the rich and diverse landscape of gender identity and expression. From understanding the complexities of various gender identities to examining the intersectionality of gender with other aspects of identity, we've delved into thought-provoking discussions and insights that challenge our preconceptions and expand our understanding of gender diversity.

Key points covered in this book include:

1. Diversity of Gender Identities: We've explored a wide range of gender identities beyond the traditional binary of male and female, including nonbinary, transgender, genderqueer, and agender identities. Each individual's experience of gender is unique and valid, and we must strive to respect and affirm people's self-identified gender identities.

2. Intersectionality and Gender: We've examined how gender intersects with other aspects of identity, such as race, sexuality, disability, and socioeconomic status, shaping individuals' experiences of privilege and oppression.

Recognizing and addressing the intersecting forms of discrimination and marginalization faced by marginalized communities is essential for creating inclusive and equitable spaces.

3. Navigating Gender in Everyday Life: We've discussed practical tips for understanding and respecting diverse gender identities in everyday interactions. From using inclusive language and challenging gender norms to advocating for inclusive policies and being allies to gender-diverse individuals, there are many ways to create inclusive environments where everyone can thrive.

4. Creating Inclusive Environments: We've explored strategies for fostering inclusivity in various settings, including workplaces, schools, and healthcare settings. By implementing inclusive policies, providing education and training, offering supportive resources and services, and fostering a culture of respect and acceptance, we can create environments where all individuals feel valued, respected, and empowered to be their authentic selves.

Understanding and respecting diverse gender identities is crucial for building a more inclusive and equitable society. By embracing the complexity and diversity of gender identity and expression, challenging systemic inequalities and discrimination, and advocating for inclusive policies and practices, we can work towards creating a world where everyone can live authentically and thrive. Let us continue to learn, grow, and advocate for gender diversity and inclusion in all aspects of our lives.

www.ingramcontent.com/pod-product-compliance
Lightning Source LLC
Chambersburg PA
CBHW061041250726

48653CB00001B/192